How Democratic Is the Constitution?

How Democratic Is the Constitution?

Robert A. Goldwin
and William A. Schambra
editors

American Enterprise Institute for Public Policy Research
Washington and London

This book is the first in a series in AEI's project "A Decade of Study of the Constitution," funded in part by a Bicentennial Challenge Grant from the National Endowment for the Humanities.

321.8042

H 83

1 1 7546

mar. 1981

Library of Congress Cataloging in Publication Data

Main entry under title:

How Democratic is the Constitution?

(AEI studies ; 294)
1. Representative government and representation—United States—Addresses, essays, lectures. 2. United States—Constitutional history—Addresses, essays, lectures. 3. Democracy—Addresses, essays, lectures. I. Goldwin, Robert A., 1922– II. Schambra, William A. III. Series: American Enterprise Institute for Public Policy Research. AEI studies ; 294.
JK21.H78   321.8′042′0973   80-24291
ISBN 0-8447-3400-4
ISBN 0-8447-3399-7 (pbk.)

AEI Studies 294

Printed in the United States of America

This volume and the series it inaugurates
are dedicated to the memory of
Martin Diamond and Herbert J. Storing

Contents

Preface *Robert A. Goldwin and William A. Schambra*

1 Democracy and the Constitution 1
    Gordon S. Wood

2 Decent, Even Though Democratic 18
    Ann Stuart Diamond

3 The Constitution as an Elitist Document 39
    Michael Parenti

4 Does the Constitution "Secure These Rights"? 59
    Walter Berns

5 Democracy and the Citizen: Community, Dignity, and
    the Crisis of Contemporary Politics in America 79
    Wilson Carey McWilliams

6 Deliberative Democracy: The Majority Principle in
    Republican Government 102
    Joseph M. Bessette

7 Conservatives, the Constitution, and the "Spirit of
    Accommodation" *Alfred F. Young* 117

The Editors and the Authors 149

Preface

When the question, How democratic is the Constitution? was answered with a resounding, Not at all, by Charles A. Beard in 1913, there resulted an intense debate among public officials, political activists, and academicians that has not subsided to this day. It is not difficult to understand why that question was and is so engaging, for it has profound implications for the way we think about and behave toward the Constitution and for the way we understand ourselves as a nation.

We profess to be a democracy, indeed, the beacon of democratic liberty throughout the world. But if Beard was correct that the Constitution is undemocratic—that it was designed to protect the wealthy by frustrating popular majorities—then there is a great discrepancy between our nation's ideals and its institutions. That discrepancy would have an important bearing on the way we understand our politics: it would seem to explain many of its complexities, frustrations, and shortcomings. And that discrepancy would have, as it had during the Progressive Era, important implications for political action and reform: Should we not seek to bring our institutions into line with our ideals by "democratizing" the Constitution through the initiative, referendum, recall, and other devices?

But if Beard was not correct—if the Constitution is in fact democratic, or if it was designed to secure rights for all through representative institutions—then we would have to understand the relationship between our ideals and institutions differently: perhaps the institutions that Beard and others have denounced as obstacles to majority rule in fact ensure that majorities rule in a sober, decent fashion. If there is a discrepancy between American ideals and institutions, it may be that our modern notions of democracy should be brought into line with "the American idea of democracy" implicit in our majority-moderating institutions.

The variety of views expressed in this volume's essays should give the reader a sense of the complexity, as well as the importance, of the question, How democratic is the Constitution? For instance, when we speak of democracy, do we mean a democracy defined by the limited equality of political rights or a democracy that demands equality in all respects? And is it instructive to compare both of these senses of democracy with an earlier sense, whereby democracy meant a kind of regime in which each citizen shared fully in the making of decisions and bore a wide range of citizenly obligations toward the community? When we speak of the "Constitution," is there a Constitution whose central meaning remains the same today as two hundred years ago, or does the Constitution's meaning change fundamentally as new times introduce new understandings? And is the question, How democratic is the Constitution? the primary one, or were the Founders right, along with those who opposed the Founders and the ratification of the Constitution, in being less concerned with democracy than with the securing of rights?

The editors selected the essays in this volume to introduce the reader to a wide range of views on these questions, presented by spokesmen as authoritative, thoughtful, and instructive as could be found. The reader should be able to make up his own mind, therefore, with the assurance that he has considered many reasonable arguments and has not simply succumbed to the orthodox view of the left or right.

Robert A. Goldwin
William A. Schambra

1

Democracy and the Constitution

Gordon S. Wood

How democratic is the Constitution? is a loaded question. It implies that the fundamental document of our national political system may be at odds with our democratic political faith. Yet, this was the central question asked at the time the Constitution was framed, and it is a question that Americans have raised ever since.

Throughout most of the nineteenth century, the Constitution's relation to democracy was usually taken for granted. In George Bancroft's view, the Constitution was the providential expression of the American people's progress toward democracy. To be sure, antebellum Southerners tried to make the Constitution their own, and some Northern abolitionists thought that the Constitution's recognition of slavery made the Constitution an abomination. The Civil War and several amendments to the Constitution cut off any serious questioning of the Constitution's democratic character. It was left to the Progressive Era at the end of the nineteenth century and beginning of the twentieth century to open up the origins of the Constitution to critical scholarly investigation and to mount a massive challenge to the identity between the Constitution and democracy.

During the last three decades of the nineteenth century, the Supreme Court declared unconstitutional a number of state laws attempting economic and social reforms. These decisions, which seemed to be frustrating the ability of the people to carry out their wishes, provoked a far-reaching debate over judicial review, the nature of the Constitution, and its relation to democracy. By the early twentieth century, this debate had generated more books and documents on the Constitution and its origins than at any other time in our history. While this controversy led some scholars to stress the importance of the rule of fundamental and natural law in

American political life, others sought to probe beneath the surface of public events and to understand judicial decisions, legislation, and constitutions not as the creations of abstract reasoning but as the products of the political process and interacting economic and social interests.[1]

The common result of these different scholarly efforts—both the insistence on the importance of natural rights and higher law in American thought and the emphasis on underlying social and economic interests in shaping law and political institutions—was to separate the Constitution from popular will and to make it something other than the natural expression of democracy. It became increasingly evident that the Constitution was not identical with what "the people" wanted but was designed through its checks and balances, difficulty of amendment, and judicial review to thwart these popular desires. Those scholars such as Edward S. Corwin and Charles G. Haines, who stressed the natural rights and higher-law background of American thinking, tried to put the best face they could on the undemocratic character of the Constitution.[2] Others, following the lead of Max Farrand, attempted to blur the issue of democracy by emphasizing the pragmatic character of the Constitution as "a bundle of compromises" designed to correct specific defects in the Articles of Confederation.[3] Many other scholars, especially after the explosive publication of Charles Beard's *An Economic Interpretation of the Constitution* in 1913, concluded outright that the Constitution was an aristocratic document, created by reactionary mercantile and creditor elements frightened by the popular agrarian tendencies of the Revolution and calculated to limit, not promote, democracy. With Beard's book, certainly the most influential history book ever written in America, the image of the Constitution could never again be quite the same.[4]

[1] For a summary of this literature, see H. Hale Bellot, "The Literature of the Last Half Century on the Constitutional History of the United States," Royal Historical Society, *Transactions*, 5th ser., vol. 7 (1957), pp. 159-82.

[2] See Edward S. Corwin, *The Doctrine of Judicial Review, Its Legal and Historical Basis, and Other Essays* (Princeton: Princeton University Press, 1914) and C. G. Haines, *The American Doctrine of Judicial Supremacy* (New York: Macmillan, 1914).

[3] Max Farrand, *The Framing of the Constitution of the United States* (New Haven: Yale University Press, 1913).

[4] Before Beard's book, the most important work arguing the undemocratic character of the Constitution was J. Allen Smith, *The Spirit of American Government, A Study of the Constitution: Its Origin, Influence and Relation to Democracy* (New York: Macmillan, 1907). For a constitutional historian's shrewd discussion of the issue on the eve of the publication of Beard's book, see Andrew C. McLaughlin, "Democracy and the Constitution," American Antiquarian Society, *Proceedings*, n.s., vol. 22 (1912), pp. 293-320.

Since World War II this Beardian or Progressive interpretation of the Constitution has been challenged in a variety of ways, and Beard's book itself has been torn to shreds. Yet the Progressive generation's historiographical achievement still casts a long shadow over much current writing about the origins of the Constitution. The issue of the Constitution's relation to democracy, once opened up by Beard and others, can no longer be taken for granted. In reaction to a half century of doubt about the democratic character of the Constitution, scholars during the past three decades have felt continually pressed to bring the Constitution within the democratic fold. They have done so largely by expanding our conception of democracy to the point where checks and balances, judicial review, and the concern for minority rights and individual liberties that once seemed antithetical to democracy have become as democratic as the majority will of popularly elected legislatures. Through this kind of expansion in the meaning of democracy, the Constitution has become for many scholars more democratic than anything it was designed to replace.

The Debate over the Constitution

The historical debate over the Constitution and democracy continues, for the debate is rooted in the original controversy that surrounded the creation of the Constitution in 1787–1788. In fact, all the historical debates over the democratic nature of the Constitution are essentially reverberations of this original dispute at the time of the framing. The creators and supporters of the Constitution, the Federalists as they called themselves, argued strenuously that the Constitution was a fulfillment, not a repudiation, of the Revolution and that it provided for a thoroughly republican and popular government. The opponents of the Constitution, the Antifederalists, charged that the Constitution was a denial of the principles of 1776 and that it was an aristocratic document calculated to create an undemocratic government benefiting the few at the expense of the many. It is essentially these two contrasting viewpoints of 1787–1788 that have been echoing through our historical writing on the origins of the Constitution ever since. We are forever trying to decide in these debates who was more right in their interpretation of the Constitution, the Federalists or the Antifederalists.

Cast in this way, the question will inevitably force us to take sides and argue that either the Federalists or the Antifederalists had a more "correct" view of the "real" Constitution. But there was and is no "real" Constitution against which we can measure the con-

3

flicting statements of the Federalists and Antifederalists. The only Constitution that existed in 1787–1788 was the one men at the time believed in and described; and these beliefs and descriptions were very different.[5] Instead of asking whether the Constitution was democratic, we should be asking what the historical participants were up to and why they described the Constitution in such different ways. When the questions are posed in this way, the answers will show that neither the Federalists nor the Antifederalists were more right in their interpretation of the Constitution; both had good reason to think as they did about the Constitution.

From the vantage point of 1776, which was generally the perspective of the Antifederalists, the Constitution of 1787 looms as an extraordinary, even unbelievable, creation. None of the revolutionary leaders at the time of independence even contemplated, let alone suggested, the possibility of erecting over all America such a strong, overarching national government as the Constitution provided. Such a powerful central government operating directly on individuals was diametrically opposed to all the principles of the Revolution. More than anything else, the Revolution intended to reduce the overweening power of the government, particularly far-removed central government associated with the British imperial system. Any revolutionary in 1776 suggesting a national government resembling the one eventually created by the Constitution of 1787 would have been branded a lunatic or, worse, a British monarchist.

The Articles of Confederation

Of course, some Americans in 1776 wanted a stronger central government than that provided by the Articles of Confederation. But

---

[5] The assertion that "there was and is no 'real' Constitution" is open to misunderstanding and criticism, which I would like to forestall. I am arguing that there was not in 1787 a single "true" or "correct" interpretation of the Constitution. The Constitution was what people thought it was; hence, the disagreement over its meaning. The continuing struggle over the meaning of the Constitution, exemplified in the essays in this volume, only substantiates my point. That struggle will never end because the "true" meaning, the "true reality" of the Constitution will never be finally discovered; no such animal exists.

It should *not* be thought that I am saying we haven't had a Constitution at all to debate. The Constitution is a very different thing from what it was in 1787, and not just because of the amendments. It can be argued that many, if not all, of these changes and additions are "illegitimate," but, if the political culture generally comes to hold them as legitimate, then for most people this changed Constitution becomes the "real" Constitution. It is because of this process of constant accretion and change that we have continuous arguments among ourselves over the meaning of the Constitution. The participants in the struggle obviously have to believe that their particular contesting interpretations are more "true" or "right" than others.

even the most fervent advocates in 1776–1777 of a stronger confederation, like John Dickinson, never envisioned a national government like that of 1787. For most revolutionaries, the confederation
was a simple political response to the need for union against Britain.
They were interested less in creating an enduring nation-state than
in legitimizing the resistance movement and the activity of the
Continental Congress. At most, they wanted a strong union of
the separate states that would have substantial authority over matters of general concern such as war, trade, interstate disputes, and
western lands. However substantial such a confederation might be,
it was still to be a confederation—a union of separate and remarkably independent states. The actual Articles of Confederation that
emerged from the congressional discussions of 1776–1777 were
weaker than some had wanted, but this limited union represented
the views of most Americans at the time.[6]

Given these American fears of far-removed central power, explaining the adoption of the Constitution in 1787–1788 becomes
quite a problem. Indeed, the formation of the Constitution seems
to be such an unexpected and unprecedented event that historians
of all persuasions have felt compelled to rely on some version of a
"great men" explanation to account for it. Some have followed
Beard and stressed the conspiratorial character of the movement
for the Constitution by a dynamic minority of nationalists who "con-
jured up" a crisis.[7] Others writing against a Beardian view have
also emphasized the youthful energy and political effectiveness of
a small group of farsighted Federalist leaders. In fact, the adulation
of recent historians for the Federalists' élan and dash has become so
great—one called them "giants in the earth"—that we may be returning to the nineteenth-century image of the Founding Fathers
as demigods.[8] Apparently the formation of the Constitution is so

---

[6] For the most recent and most persuasive account of the Confederation Congress,
see Jack N. Rakove, *The Beginnings of National Politics: An Interpretative
History of the Continental Congress* (New York: Knopf, 1979).

[7] See E. James Ferguson, *The Power of the Purse: A History of American Public
Finance, 1776–1790* (Chapel Hill: University of North Carolina Press, 1961), p. 337;
Merrill Jensen, *The New Nation: A History of the United States, 1781–1789* (New
York: Knopf, 1950), pp. 348–49; and Jackson Turner Main, *The Antifederalists:
Critics of the Constitution, 1781–1788* (Chapel Hill: University of North Carolina
Press, 1961), pp. 177–78.

[8] See Stanley Elkins and Eric McKitrick, "The Founding Fathers: Young Men of
the Revolution," *Political Science Quarterly*, vol. 76 (1961), pp. 181–216; John P.
Roche, "The Founding Fathers: A Reform Caucus in Action," *American Political
Science Review*, vol. 55 (1961), pp. 799–816; Robert A. Rutland, *Ordeal of the
Constitution: The Antifederalists and the Ratification Struggle of 1787–1788*

inexplicable that it cannot be accounted for except in terms of the heroic actions of a few great men.

Of course, many historians have described the accumulating problems of the confederation in order to explain the writing of the Constitution. Although no one today endorses John Fiske's view that the decade of the 1780s was "the most critical moment in all the history of the American people"—a time of near chaos and anarchy—historians have pointed out that the confederation was suffering from a number of visible weaknesses.[9] In international affairs, the confederation was hard-pressed to maintain its territorial integrity. Great Britain refused to vacate the Northwest posts; Spain claimed a huge chunk of the Southwest and closed the Mississippi to traffic. The Barbary pirates were seizing American ships and crews because Congress had no money to pay the necessary tributes. Lacking any taxing power, the United States government could not even pay the interest on its debt to its creditors at home or abroad. Congress had no authority to regulate commerce and thus had no way of forcing any openings in the European mercantile empires for American traders. Efforts to get even limited taxing and commercial regulatory powers foundered on the requirements for the unanimous consent of all the states for amendment of the Articles of Confederation.

Pressing and serious as these problems of the confederation were, they cannot by themselves explain the formation of the Constitution. The Constitution created a national government whose strength and character were out of proportion to the obvious and acknowledged weaknesses of the confederation. Indeed, by 1787 almost everyone recognized the debility of the Articles and was prepared to grant additional powers to Congress. They were not prepared for what came out of the Philadelphia Convention of 1787— a revolutionary transformation of the entire American political system including a radical diminishing of the independence and power of the states. This was no invigorated league of states that the Constitution created. This totally new and extraordinarily powerful national government operating directly on individuals went well beyond what the difficulties of credit and commerce and the humiliations in foreign affairs demanded in additional central powers.

(Norman: University of Oklahoma Press, 1966); and Forrest McDonald, *E Pluribus Unum: The Formation of the American Republic, 1776-1790* (Boston: Houghton Mifflin, 1965), p. 236.

[9] John Fiske, *The Critical Period of American History* (New York: Houghton Mifflin, 1888), p. 55.

The Problem of Democracy in the States

Something besides the obvious debility of the confederation lay behind such a radical political transformation. Only political conditions in the states—political conditions of the most threatening kind—can ultimately explain the creation of the Constitution. There in the states, the political entities the revolutionaries cared about most, the problem of democracy was revealed; and it is that problem the Constitution sought to solve.

The state republics created in 1776 were at the heart of the Revolution. Winning the war and forming the Articles of Confederation were crucial, no doubt, but creating new state constitutions, as Thomas Jefferson said in 1776, was "the whole object of the present controversy." In their new commonwealths, Americans aimed to test all that they had learned about tyranny and liberty from their colonial experience and their debate with Britain in the 1760s and 1770s. Republicanism and popular government in America, and indeed in the world, would live or die by what happened in these individual states.[10]

In 1776 Americans as yet did not call their new governments democracies; it is important for our understanding of the Constitution's relationship to democracy to know why they did not. It is true that the new state governments were very popular, more popular surely than any other government in the eighteenth-century world. In the American states, a greater proportion of people could vote and a greater proportion of government officials were elected than in any other country. The most popular part of the state governments, the lower houses of the legislatures, were given an extraordinary amount of power, including many prerogatives, like the granting of pardons and the appointment of judges, that were traditionally exercised only by magisterial authority in other countries. Still, these new governments were not called democracies because, as the eighteenth century commonly understood the term, they were *not* democracies.

Americans in 1776 thought of democracy in a traditionally classical manner. Democracy was not what it has become for us—a general set of values embracing popular government, equality, and liberty. It was still a rather technical term of political science used much as Aristotle had used it. It meant literally government by the people,

---

[10] For the importance of the state constitutions to the Revolution of 1776, see Gordon S. Wood, *The Creation of the American Republic, 1776-1787* (Chapel Hill: University of North Carolina Press, 1969), pp. 127-255.

referring in the strictest sense to political gatherings of the people in person in town meetings and the like. Since such pure democracy was impractical for most governmental affairs, Americans recognized as democratic the modern refinement of representation, which allowed elected agents to participate in government in place of the people. Representation was not yet equated, as it is now, with mere popular election. The representatives of the people were exclusively those elected members of the lower houses of the legislatures—the houses of representatives. The officials of the other branches of the government—whether governors or senators—even though elected by the people, were not yet considered to be in any way "representatives" of the people. They stood "for" the people but were not "of" them. Thus, any state that possessed a governor and a senate, although popularly elected, could not be a democracy. Americans in 1776 therefore saw themselves creating mixed republics, with the democratic element, the lower assemblies, playing a very dominant role.

By the 1780s, many American leaders realized that these state assemblies were abusing their extraordinary powers. The annually elected legislatures, beset by hosts of various interests, were constantly changing their membership and were making legislation chaotic. As James Madison pointed out, more laws were enacted by the states in the decade following independence than in the entire colonial period. Many of these laws were unjust: paper money acts, stay laws, and other forms of debtor relief legislation hurt various creditor groups in the society and violated individual property rights. To some, the legislatures seemed more frightening than the former royal governors. It did not matter that the legislators were supposedly the representatives of the people and annually elected by them. "173 despots would surely be as oppressive as one," wrote Jefferson. "An *elective despotism* was not the government we fought for."[11]

These legislative abuses, many American leaders believed, flowed from too much democracy. The legislators were too susceptible to various narrow and parochial interests and had become merely spokesmen for their local constituents. "A spirit of locality" in the state legislatures, said Madison, was destroying "the aggregate interests of the Community," and this localist spirit was "inseparable" from elections by small districts or towns. Each representative, said Ezra Stiles, president of Yale, was concerned only with the special interests of his electors. At the reading of a bill in the legislature, "every one

---

[11] Thomas Jefferson, *Notes on the State of Virginia*, ed. William Peden (Chapel Hill: University of North Carolina Press, 1955), p. 120.

instantly thinks how it will affect his constituents."[12] In short, the representatives of the people—the democratic parts of the mixed constitutions—were responding too readily to the wishes of the people they represented. When the Federalists in 1787 came to complain of "the turbulence and follies of democracy," this is what they meant.[13]

American leaders tried several approaches to these democratic abuses in the states. Some attempted to reform the revolutionary state constitutions by reducing the power of the popular assemblies and enhancing that of the governors and senates. The Massachusetts constitution of 1780 embodied many of these second thoughts, and during the 1780s other states sought to remake their constitutions in Massachusetts' image. Others tried to use the judiciary against what were thought to be unconstitutional acts of the legislatures; there were scattered and rudimentary expressions of what would become judicial review. Many leaders, however, thought such judicial over-turnings of law enacted by popularly elected legislatures smacked of despotism and were contrary to republican government.

By the mid-1780s, men were increasingly disillusioned with these reforms and devices at the state level. Finally, when even Massachusetts with its supposedly model constitution experienced popular excesses, including Shays' Rebellion and the subsequent legislative "tyranny" of Shaysite sympathizers, many leaders were ready to shift the arena of constitutional change from the states to the nation. It seemed to many that only by modifying the structure of the central government could America find an answer to its democratically caused problems within the states.

What happened in 1786–1787, in brief, was the coalescing of two different and hitherto separate reform movements. The previously frustrated attempts of various groups—public creditors, merchants, and others—to amend the Articles of Confederation were reinforced by the efforts of those alarmed by majoritarian tyranny within the states. Heightened concern with the implications of state politics overwhelmed the state particularism and the fear of far-removed central power that had prevented earlier reform of the Articles of Confederation and forced a recasting of the terms of the problem

---

[12] Madison's observations on Jefferson's draft of a constitution for Virginia (1788), Julian P. Boyd, ed., *The Papers of Thomas Jefferson* (Princeton: Princeton University Press, 1950-), vol. 6, pp. 308-09; Ezra Stiles, "The United States Elevated to Glory and Honor . . ." (New Haven, 1783), in John W. Thornton, ed., *The Pulpit of the American Revolution* . . . (Boston: Gould and Lincoln, 1860), p. 420.

[13] Edmund Randolph in Max Farrand, ed., *The Records of the Federal Convention* (New Haven: Yale University Press, 1937), vol. 1, p. 51.

facing Americans. Since the legislative abuses of the states flowed from the revolutionary aim of increasing the participation of the people in government, the very success of the revolutionary experiment in popular government was at stake. Thus, changing the central government was no longer a matter of standing firm in foreign affairs or of satisfying particular creditor or mercantile interests. It was now a matter, as Madison said, that would "decide forever the fate of republican government."[14]

An Enlarged and Elevated Republic

No one saw this linkage between reform of the central government and reform of the states more clearly and used it more effectively than Madison. Nearly everyone is familiar with Madison's central role in planning for the Philadelphia Convention and in drafting the Virginia plan, which was the convention's working proposal. But not everyone is equally familiar with what Madison wanted from the new central government and how disappointed he was with the final Constitution. Madison's proposals were truly radical; they were designed not to solve particular problems of the confederation but to remedy the deficiencies of republicanism itself. The evidence is strong that Madison and other nationalists who thought like him wanted greater consolidation and a correspondingly greater weakening of the states than they got. Madison wanted a national government that not only would have "a positive and compleat authority in all cases where uniform measures are necessary," as in commerce and foreign policy, but would have "a negative in all cases whatsoever on the Legislative Acts of the States as the King of Great Britain heretofore had." This veto power over all state legislation seemed to Madison "to be absolutely necessary, and to be the least possible encroachment on the State jurisdictions."[15] Without it, he believed, none of the great objects which led to the convention—neither the need for more central authority nor the desire to prevent instability and injustice in state legislation—would be met. When the convention eventually set aside this national veto power, Madison initially thought that the Constitution was doomed to failure.[16]

---

[14] Madison quoted in Charles Warren, *The Making of the Constitution* (Cambridge, Massachusetts: Harvard University Press, 1947), p. 82.

[15] Madison to Edmund Randolph, April 8, 1787, Robert A. Rutland et al., eds., *The Papers of James Madison* (Chicago: University of Chicago Press, 1962-), vol. 9, p. 370; Madison to George Washington, April 16, 1787, ibid., vol. 9, p. 383.

[16] For a recent discussion of Madison's national veto, see Charles F. Hobson, "The Negative on State Laws: James Madison and the Crisis of Republican Government," *William and Mary Quarterly*, 3rd ser., vol. 36 (1979), pp. 215-35.

Although deeply disappointed with the Constitution, Madison and other nationalists aimed to make the best of what they had, a greatly enlarged and elevated republic. All scholars now know how ingeniously Madison made theoretical sense of the new national system. Seizing on David Hume's radical suggestion that a republican government might operate better in a large territory than in a small one, Madison reversed the traditional assumptions about the appropriate size of a republic. Since experience in America from 1776 had demonstrated that no republic could be made small enough to avoid the clashing of rival parties and interests (tiny Rhode Island was the most faction-ridden of all), the republican state, said Madison in a series of notable letters, essays, and speeches climaxing with his *Federalist* No. 10, must be enlarged "without a departure from the elective basis of it." In this way "the propensity in small republics to rash measures and the facility of forming and executing them" by overbearing factional majorities would be stifled. "In a large Society," said Madison, "the people are broken into so many interests and parties, that a common sentiment is less likely to be felt, and the requisite concert less likely to be formed, by a majority of the whole."[17]

All this may be common knowledge to scholars, but it has led to great misunderstanding of Madison's meaning. Some have pictured Madison as the originator of what has come to be called an "interest-group" theory of politics. But Madison was not a forerunner of Arthur Bentley, David Truman, or Robert Dahl. Despite his keen appreciation of the multiplicity of interests in a commercial society, Madison was not presenting a pluralist conception of politics. He did not envision public policy or the common good emerging naturally from the give-and-take of hosts of competing interests.[18] Instead he hoped that these competing parties and interests in an enlarged republic would neutralize themselves, which in turn would allow rational men to promote the public good. It had worked that way in America's religious situation, which was a common analogy for Madison. The multiplicity of religious sects in America prevented any from dominating the state and permitted the enlightened reason of *philosophes* like Jefferson and himself to shape public policy and

---

17 *The Federalist*, ed. Jacob E. Cooke (Middletown, Connecticut: Wesleyan University Press, 1961), No. 10; Madison to Jefferson, October 24, 1787, Rutland et al., eds., *Madison Papers*, vol. 10, p. 214.

18 On this point, see Robert J. Morgan, "Madison's Theory of Representation in the Tenth *Federalist*," *Journal of Politics*, vol. 36 (1974), pp. 852-85; and Paul F. Bourke, "The Pluralist Reading of James Madison's Tenth *Federalist*," *Perspectives in American History*, vol. 9 (1975), pp. 271-95.

church-state relations. Madison did not want the new national government to be an integrator and harmonizer of different interests in the society; instead he wanted it to be a "disinterested and dispassionate umpire in disputes" between these different interests.[19] In other words, Madison was not as modern as we often make him out to be. He hoped the national government might play the same role the British king had been supposed to play in the empire.

Cosmopolitanism vs. Localism

If the new government were to be monarchlike with its own "dispassionate and disinterested" authority, how was it to work in republican America? "It may be asked," Madison said, "how private rights will be more secure under the Guardianship of the General Government than under the State Governments, since they are both founded on the republican principle which refers the ultimate decision to the will of the majority."[20] What, in other words, was really different about the new federal Constitution from the state constitutions that would enable it to lessen the effects of tyrannical majorities and keep it from succumbing to the same popular pressures besetting the state governments in the 1780s?

The answer the Federalists gave to these questions cut to the heart of the new system and reveals clearly the problem of the Constitution's relation to democracy. The Federalists, Madison included, were not as much opposed to governmental power per se as to the character and outlook of the people wielding it. They thought that the vices of the state assemblies in the 1780s flowed essentially from the kinds of people being elected to these assemblies. Such legislators were too often too much like the people they represented.

The Revolution had democratized the state assemblies by increasing the number of representatives and by altering their social character. Men of more humble, more rural origins, less educated, and with more parochial interests than those in the colonial legislatures became state representatives after 1776. These nongentry elements formed what Jackson Turner Main has called "localist parties" in all the state legislatures.[21] Although the turnover of membership among these groups was perhaps too great to permit such a rigid classification as

---

[19] Madison to Washington, April 16, 1787, Rutland et al., eds., *Madison Papers*, vol. 9, p. 384.

[20] Madison to Jefferson, October 24, 1787, Rutland et al., eds., *Madison Papers*, vol. 10, p. 212.

[21] Jackson Turner Main, *Political Parties before the Constitution* (Chapel Hill: University of North Carolina Press, 1973).

"party," these legislative blocs took consistently localist positions on many issues that their cosmopolitan elite opponents criticized as "illiberal," "interested," and "unprincipled." Madison and other gentlemen believed that these ordinary men lacked the "enlarged" and "liberal" outlooks of the more cosmopolitan "natural aristocracy" that Jefferson, for one, had expected to dominate government. These ordinary men were the ones winning elections to the state legislatures and enacting most of what the Federalists described as the confused, unjust, and narrowly based legislation of the 1780s. What the Federalists wanted from the Constitution was a structure of government that would inhibit such localist kinds of men from gaining power.

They proposed to do this by enlarging the arena of politics. Raising important governmental decision making to the national level would expand the electorate and at the same time would reduce the number of those elected. This expanded electorate and elevated government would then act as a kind of filter, refining the kind of men who would become national leaders. In a larger arena with a smaller number of representatives, only the most notable and most socially established were likely to gain political office. If the people of a state, New York, for example, had to select only ten men to the federal Congress in contrast to the sixty-six they elected to their state assembly, they were more apt in the case of the few representatives in the national government to ignore obscure ordinary men with local reputations and elect those who were well bred, well educated, and well known. Election by the people in large districts would inhibit demagoguery and crass electioneering and would therefore, as Madison's closest ally in the convention, James Wilson, said, "be most likely to obtain men of intelligence and uprightness."[22]

What was the meaning of all this Federalist talk of keeping out of government "men of factious tempers, of localist prejudices, or of sinister designs"? Who were the men possessing "the most attractive merit and most diffusive and established characters"?[23] If anyone today used those terms to describe political leaders, we would be understandably suspicious. We might even say that these are "code words" for distinct social types. The Federalist diagnosis of the problems of state politics in the 1780s was at bottom social. Prior to the Revolution, the colonists, like all eighteenth-century Englishmen, had less need for such circumlocutions; they then talked more candidly about the distinction between gentlemen and ordinary people and

---

[22] Wilson in Farrand, ed., *Records of the Federal Convention*, vol. 1, p. 154. The first Congress had only sixty-five representatives, smaller than most of the state assemblies at that time.

[23] *The Federalist* No. 10.

were much more blunt in designating some as aristocrats and most as not. Since the Revolution, however, the distinction between gentlemen and common people was becoming blurred; aristocracy, even a republican "natural aristocracy," had become a pejorative term in many parts of the country. It is perhaps anachronistic and crude to refer to this gentry sense of difference from obscure ordinary people as a "class" distinction, for it was a distinction that belonged to the older hierarchically and vertically organized society of ranks and degrees and not to the economically based class and horizontally organized society of the future. Yet, it is surely more accurate to describe the controversy over the Constitution in these anachronistic and crude "class" terms than to suggest that it had no social implications whatsoever. The Federalists knew well the social significance of their enlarged republic. They had a shrewd sociological insight into American politics, and they aimed to use it in transforming the social character of American government.

It is a sociological insight that was exploited time and again in later American history. The Progressive period, for example, was marked by the reforming efforts of cosmopolitan types, often liberal, upper-income professionals and businessmen, to wrest the reins of government out of the hands of "corrupt" and "undesirable" localist elements. The Progressive reformers often did this by shifting the level of governmental decision making from wards, towns, and counties to the states and the nation. Commissions of "experts" at the state and federal level supplanted parochial politicians who could not see beyond their own neighborhoods.[24] Changing the level of decision making continues to have social implications; much of our national politics still swirls around this cosmopolitan-localist dichotomy. What do we mean socially when we refer to "establishment types," "limousine liberals," "Middle America," or "Archie Bunkers"?

A Republican Remedy for Republican Diseases

Whether such cosmopolitan efforts to create political structures that deliberately excluded the ordinariness of ordinary people are undemocratic was precisely the issue raised at the framing of the Constitution. The Antifederalists, speaking for a populist localist tradition, certainly thought the Constitution was undemocratic. They immediately saw the social implications of the elevated federal government,

---

[24] See especially Samuel P. Hays, "Political Parties and the Community-Society Continuum," in William Nisbet Chambers and Walter Dean Burnham, eds., *The American Party Systems: Stages of Political Development* (New York: Oxford University Press, 1967), pp. 152-81.

where only certain "high-toned" and "great men" would hold office and consequently attacked it as "aristocratic" and contrary to the aim of the Revolution.

Yet, the issue has always been complicated by the fact that the Federalists did not allow themselves to be pictured as opposed to the people or republicanism. They had good reason to know that the Constitution would be seen as undemocratic. "When this plan goes forth," John Dickinson warned the Philadelphia Convention, "it will be attacked by the popular leaders. Aristocracy will be the watchword; the Shibboleth among its adversaries." Precisely because the Antifederalists, as Alexander Hamilton observed in the New York ratifying convention, did talk "so often of an aristocracy," the Federalists were compelled in the ratifying debates and in their publications to minimize, even to disguise, the elitist elements of the Constitution.[25] Much of *The Federalist*, for example, was devoted to demonstrating just how "strictly republican" the new system was.[26] The Federalists emerged from the debates, if we take their public statements at face value, as the great defenders of the supremacy of the people in politics. They said over and over again that the new national government, unlike the old confederation, was fully derived from the people. The states could not stand in the way of what the people wanted, and the Constitution was only fulfilling at the national level what the Revolution in 1776 had begun. In effect, the Federalists usurped the popular revolutionary language that rightfully belonged to their opponents and, in the process, helped to further the extraordinary changes taking place in the American conception of politics and democracy.

By the end of the debate over the Constitution, it was possible for the Federalists to describe the new national government, even with its indirectly elected president and Senate, as "a perfectly democratical form of government."[27] Already by 1787–1788 democracy had come to be identified by some Americans simply as a representative government derived from the people. In other words, republicanism and democracy were becoming equated. The houses of representatives lost

---

[25] Dickinson in Farrand, ed., *Records of the Federal Convention*, vol. 2, p. 278; Hamilton in Jonathan Elliot, ed., *The Debates of the Several State Conventions on the Adoption of the Federal Constitution* (Philadelphia: Lippincott, 1876), vol. 2, p. 256.

[26] See especially Martin Diamond, "Democracy and *The Federalist*: A Reconsideration of the Framers' Intent," *American Political Science Review*, vol. 53 (1959), pp. 52-68, and Diamond, "The Federalist, 1787-1788," in Leo Strauss and Joseph Cropsey, eds., *History of Political Philosophy* (Chicago: Rand McNally, 1963), pp. 573-93.

[27] Nathaniel Gorham (Massachusetts) in Elliot, ed., *Debates*, vol. 2, p. 69.

their exclusive connection with the people. Representation was now identified simply with election; thus, all elected officials, and, for some, even those not elected, such as judges, were considered somehow "representative" of the people. Consequently, the older classical ideas of democracy and mixed government that went back to Aristotle became irrelevant in describing the new American political system. Democracy rapidly became a generic label for all American government.

The changes in language and thought that made this new, more modern definition of democracy possible were not as easily reached as suggested here. Nor was the Federalist use of populism to defend the Constitution as self-conscious or calculating as here implied. Ideas and words are not manipulated or transformed quite that crudely. But, in sum, the Federalists did seek to cover their aristocratic document with a democratic mantle. The state problems of the 1780s they hoped to solve were those of excessive democracy; yet, the solution, they said, or felt compelled to say, was likewise democratic. As Madison, who was somewhat less willing than other Federalists to distort language and indulge the people, put it, the Constitution was "a republican remedy for the diseases most incident to republican government."[28] Whatever the terms used, the Federalists in their public statements were not able to say candidly what at least some had said within the secrecy of the Philadelphia Convention: that the source of their difficulties came from too much local democracy, and that the solution was to limit this local democracy by erecting a more aristocratic structure over it.

In the end, the Federalists had little choice in their rhetoric. If they were to get the Constitution ratified, they had to work within the egalitarian and populist currents flowing from the Revolution. Despite the suggestion of disingenuousness, there is no denying their achievement. They thought and acted more creatively than any other generation in American history. They not only convinced the country to accept a national government inconceivable a decade earlier but they did so without repudiating the republicanism and the popular basis of government that nearly all devoutly believed in. The Federalists of 1787–1788 were not the Federalists of the 1790s; they were alarmed by the abuses of popular power, but they were not, like the later Federalist party, actually fearful of the people. They remained

---

[28] *The Federalist* No. 10. Madison's careful distinction between a republic, "in which the scheme of representation takes place," and a democracy, where the people "assemble and administer the government in person," was not supported by many Federalists. Before long all American governments were being called "representative democracies." See Wood, *Creation of the American Republic*, pp. 593-96.

confident that, if only the people's choice could be undisturbed by ambitious local demagogues and crass electioneering, the people would "choose men of the first character for wisdom and integrity," men very much like themselves.[29] It was an achievement that transcended their intentions and one that has rightly earned them the admiration of subsequent generations. Somehow for a moment they reconciled aristocracy with democracy and gave us, as John P. Roche has said, "a classic example of the potentialities of a democratic elite."[30]

Nevertheless, great as the Federalists' achievement was, the cost to the future of American politics was high. By using the most popular and democratic rhetoric available to explain and justify their aristocratic system, the Federalists helped to foreclose the development of an American intellectual tradition in which differing ideas of politics would be intimately and genuinely related to differing social interests. In other words, the Federalists of 1787 furthered the American disavowal of any sort of aristocratic conception of politics and encouraged the American belief that the ills of democracy can be cured by more democracy. From the creation of the Constitution, as the Federalist party of the 1790s eventually discovered to its dismay, democracy in America was no longer something to be discussed skeptically and challenged but a faith to which all Americans and all American institutions must unquestioningly adhere.

---

[29] *Hartford, Connecticut Courant*, February 5, 1787.
[30] Roche, "The Founding Fathers," p. 816.

2

Decent, Even Though Democratic

Ann Stuart Diamond

If the republican form is, as all of us agree, to be preferred, the final question must be, what is the structure of it that will best guard against precipitate counsels and factious combinations for unjust purposes, without a sacrifice of the fundamental principle of Republicanism.

[N]o government of human device and human administration can be perfect ... that which is the least imperfect is therefore the best government ... the abuses of all other governments have led to the preference of republican government as the best of all governments, because the least imperfect; [and] the vital principle of republican government is the lex majoris partis, *the will of the majority. ...*

James Madison, 1834

How democratic is the Constitution? Perhaps some clarification of terms will be helpful as a prelude to answering this question. Exactly what is a democratic constitution? Three obstacles impede agreement on the essentials of a democratic constitution. First, the modern success of utopianism interposes between us and the American founding a radical theory of democracy that, among other things, rests on a belief in the perfectibility of man by means of the right political and social institutions.[1] Second, Americans have no way to understand

---

NOTE: The author wishes to acknowledge a great debt to William Schambra's counsel in the preparation of this essay.

[1] Irving Kristol, *Two Cheers for Capitalism* (New York: Basic Books, 1978), p. 159. Kristol explains that the crucial difference between ancient and modern utopianism is that the latter regards utopias as ideals to be actually realized—in this case, to transform man's nature. See also Martin Diamond, "The Utopian Grounds for Pessimism and the Reasonable Grounds for Optimism," in *Causes for Optimism* (Rockford, Ill.: Rockford College, 1973), p. 46.

what aristocracy really means—Tocqueville is an invaluable guide
here—for we have never had any real experience of aristocracy. Our
lack of any aristocratic tradition accounts both for suspicions that it
lurks everywhere, particularly in the eighteenth-century origins of the
American polity, and for the error of mistaking for an aristocratic
manifestation whatever slows the expression of the majority will.[2]
The third obstacle is the problem of correctly interpreting the founders' "cool acceptance" of democratic government. Equal emphasis
must be placed on "cool" and on "acceptance." Nowhere is this
treated more profoundly than in the work of Martin Diamond[3] (the
details of his analysis will be considered later). Here it is important
to see why this is an obstacle to agreement on what qualified as a
democratic constitution. In a sentence, we do not acknowledge as
democratic a view of democracy that treats it as a problem, rather
than as an unqualified good.

With these obstacles in mind, let us now consider James Madison's definition of a democratic constitution, found primarily in *The
Federalist*.[4] In *Federalist* No. 10, he distinguished between a "pure
democracy" and a "republic" and in so doing gave to the concept of
republic "an exclusively democratic content":[5]

> [By] pure democracy, I mean a society, consisting of a small
> number of citizens, who assemble and administer the gov-
> ernment in person. . . .

> [By] a republic I mean a government in which the scheme
> of representation takes place. . . .

---

[2] Tocqueville observed that Americans were unique in being "born equal." In
chapter 2, volume 1 of *Democracy in America*, Phillips Bradley, ed. (New York:
Knopf, 1945), he explained, "land is the basis of an aristocracy . . . for it is not by
privileges alone, nor by birth, but by landed property handed down from generation to generation, that an aristocracy is constituted." He rightly emphasized
that laws of inheritance in America have operated to destroy this possibility.

[3] See for example: "Democracy and *The Federalist*: A Reconsideration of the
Framers' Intent," *American Political Science Review*, vol. 53 (1959); "Conservatives, Liberals and the Constitution," in Robert A. Goldwin, ed., *Left, Right and
Center* (Chicago: Rand McNally, 1967); "The Revolution of Sober Expectations,"
in *America's Continuing Revolution* (Washington, D.C.: American Enterprise
Institute, 1975); and "The Declaration and the Constitution: Liberty, Democracy,
and the Founders," *Public Interest*, no. 39 (1975).

[4] Samuel Johnson's eighteenth-century dictionary defines democracy as "one of
three forms of government; that in which the sovereign power is lodged in the
body of the people." The eleventh edition of the *Encyclopaedia Britannica* says
"that form of government in which the people rules itself, either directly or
indirectly, as in small city-states in Greece, or through representatives."

[5] Martin Diamond, "The Federalist," in Leo Strauss and Joseph Cropsey, eds.,
History of Political Philosophy (Chicago: Rand McNally, 1963), p. 579.

The two great points of difference between a democracy and a republic, are first, the delegation of the government, in the latter, to a small number of citizens elected by the rest; secondly, the greater number of citizens, and greater sphere of the country, over which the latter may be extended.[6]

Then, in *Federalist* No. 14, Madison wrote:

The true distinction between these [democratic and republican] forms . . . is, that in a democracy, the people meet and exercise the government in person; in a republic they assemble and administer it by their representatives and agents.

Again, in *Federalist* No. 39, he stated:

The first question that offers itself is, whether the general form and aspect of the government be strictly republican? It is evident that no other form would be reconcilable with the genius of the people of America; with the fundamental principles of the revolution; or with that honorable determination, which animates every votary of freedom, to rest all our political experiments on the capacity of mankind for self-government.

In trying to define the republican form, Madison ruled out reference to other political writers, because of "extreme inaccuracy with which the term has been used in political disquisitions." For example, Holland had been described as a republic, yet no part of ultimate political authority derived from the people; Venice, also called a republic, located supreme power in the hands of a small number of hereditary nobles. Poland, a combination of the "worst forms" of aristocracy and monarchy, was likewise described; finally, England, with only one republican branch, was often listed among republics.

A Democratic Republic

Madison, therefore, carefully developed the new, wholly popular definition of republicanism that he introduced in *Federalist* No. 10:

[W]e may define a republic to be, or at least may bestow that name on, a government which derives all its powers directly or indirectly from the great body of the people; and is administered by persons holding their offices during pleasure, for a limited period, or during good behavior. It is *essential* to such a government, that it be derived from the

---

[6] In contrast, Johnson defines a republic as a "commonwealth; state in which the power is lodged in more than one."

great body of society, not from an inconsiderable proportion, or a favored class of it; . . . It is *sufficient* for such a government, that the persons administering it be appointed, either directly or indirectly, by the people; and that they hold their appointments by either of the tenures just specified; otherwise every government in the United States, as well as every other popular government that has been or can be well organized or well executed would be degraded from the republican character.[7]

A republic, then and henceforth, is a representative democracy. Both a republic and a democracy belong to that class of government named *popular*, government that includes all "forms of rule by the many, as distinguished from the various forms of rule by the few or the one."[8] In fact, the terms *republic, democracy,* and *popular government* are used interchangeably in *The Federalist,* at the federal convention, and in the correspondence of both Madison and Hamilton.[9] Madison uses republic to mean government by the majority throughout his writings.[10] The blurring of the distinction between a republic and a democracy is often ignored by critics of the Constitution, who point triumphantly to the founders' arguments for the "republican form" as conclusive evidence of their antidemocratic intentions. Friends of the Constitution, who argue that the founders' sober republicanism stands in sharp contrast to, and as a vast improvement over, the radical democracy of our times, make a similar mistake, though for a very different reason.

In simplest terms, a democratic constitution can be defined as one in which the will of the majority prevails, or in which the majority rules. Whether this rule is exercised directly (pure democracy) or indirectly (representative democracy or republic), the principle is the same: Both forms of rule rest on the "capacity of mankind for self-government." Notice, however, that this basic definition does not require liberty but does require political equality. In other words,

---

[7] Alexander Hamilton, James Madison, and John Jay, *The Federalist,* Clinton Rossiter, ed. (New York: New American Library, Mentor Books, 1961). Madison reminded his readers that the Constitution guarantees to each state a republican form of government. This has always been understood to mean a democratic form of government.

[8] Martin Diamond, "The Federalist," p. 580.

[9] Ibid.

[10] See, for example, "Vices of the Political System of the United States," Robert Rutland and William M. E. Rachal, eds., *The Papers of James Madison,* vol. 9 (Charlottesville: University of Virginia Press, 1975), p. 355; "James Madison's Autobiography," Douglass Adair, ed., *The William and Mary Quarterly,* 3rd ser., vol. 2 (April 1945), p. 208; and the quotations that open this essay.

majority rule is compatible with nonliberty, as the prefounding history of majority or democratic rule taught. That had been the problem of democracy.

In the remainder of the essay, I will attempt to show that the answer to the question—how democratic is the constitution?—is that it is entirely so. To demonstrate this, I will examine the relationship between the Declaration of Independence and the Constitution, the act of founding, the institutions created thereby, and the political behavior generated by those institutions. This is the teaching of Martin Diamond's work on the founding. If, as Diamond and I believe, the Constitution is wholly democratic by intention, perhaps we may conclude the essay by asking, *why* be democratic?

But the common view is not at all that the Constitution is entirely democratic. The Constitution is considered a conservative document, intended to protect the privileges (or "liberty") of the propertied classes, against the sentiments and actions inspired by that "democratic manifesto," the Declaration of Independence. In this view, the Declaration is "thought to proclaim a democratic regime in which government functions by consent of the governed in such a way as to secure a free society."[11] This is almost the exact reverse of the way the founders understood their handiwork; a sober rereading of the Declaration supports them. The Declaration established the criteria for the ends of legitimate government and thereby made the compelling case that a people have a right to their own government. Following the teaching of John Locke, the only legitimate end for government became the securing of liberty:

> We hold these Truths to be self-evident, that all Men are created equal, that they are endowed by their Creator with certain unalienable Rights, that among these are Life, Liberty and the Pursuit of Happiness—That to secure these Rights, Governments are instituted among Men, deriving their just Powers from the Consent of the Governed, that whenever any Form of Government becomes destructive of these Ends, it is the Right of the People to alter or abolish it, and to institute new Government, laying its Foundations on such principles, and organizing its Powers in such Form, as to them shall seem most likely to effect their Safety and Happiness.

The phrases "created equal" and "consent of the governed" are now understood within a "horizon of egalitarian democracy" instead

---

11 Martin Diamond, Winston M. Fisk, and Herbert Garfinkel, *The Democratic Republic* (Chicago: Rand McNally, 1970), 2d ed., p. 5.

of in the context of their adoption—the "horizon of liberty of the founding generation" (in Diamond's words).[12] That is what misleads us. "Equal" in the Declaration does not mean the egalitarianism, the human equality in all things, that so dominates contemporary thinking. In Jefferson's original draft, the actual meaning is quite clear: All men are "created equal and independent" and from that "equal creation they derive rights inherent and inalienable." "Independent" refers to the condition of man before he enters into political society. "The social contract theory upon which the Declaration is based teaches not equality as such but equal political liberty."[13] Men are born into a state of nature in which they are absolutely independent of every other man. In John Locke's theory (from which the Declaration draws heavily), this equal independence gives each perfect freedom from the other. Leaving the state of nature to enter political society, men give up their equal perfect freedom for equal "unalienable rights" in civil society. Equality as it is described in the Declaration is the "equal entitlement of all to the rights which comprise political liberty, and nothing more."[14] Here we can look to Lincoln for clarification: "The authors of that notable instrument . . . did not intend to declare all men equal in all respects. They did not mean to say all were equal in color, size, intellect, moral developments, or social capacity. They defined with tolerable distinctness, in what respects they did consider all men created equal—equal in 'certain unalienable rights, among which are life, liberty, and the pursuit of happiness.' "[15]

The Declaration does not say that a government shall be instituted that *operates* by consent of the governed, that is, democratic government. Instead, the Declaration argues that consent is necessary to institute or establish a government on principles chosen by the governed. The document is silent as to the form of government adequate to secure these unalienable rights. Indeed, one acceptable form was to be found in England, whose mixed or balanced government was universally admired as the freest government in history. Writing to Thomas Jefferson in 1825, James Madison characterized the Declaration thus to its author:

---

[12] This discussion of the meaning of the Declaration of Independence is taken from Martin Diamond, "The Declaration and the Constitution: Liberty, Democracy, and the Founders," Nathan Glazer and Irving Kristol, eds., *The American Commonwealth, 1976* (New York: Basic Books, 1975), pp. 48ff.

[13] Ibid., p. 49.

[14] Ibid.

[15] Ibid.

Sydney and Locke are admirably calculated to impress on young minds the right of nations to establish their own governments, and to inspire a love of free ones, but afford no aid in guarding our Republican charters against constructive violations. The Declaration of Independence, tho rich in fundamental principles, and saying everything that could be said in the same number of words, falls really under a like observation.[16]

Madison was saying that the Declaration teaches the right to one's own government and the love for free government but that it contains no principles enabling like-minded men to protect republican (democratic) charters from being construed or administered into a different form of government. Jefferson found nothing to disagree with in this. Both men would concur in my analysis thus far—that the Declaration is a most powerful statement against colonial rule and for free governments, those whose end is liberty.

Securing Liberty

The Declaration offers no guidance as how best to secure liberty. "Any form is legitimate, provided it secures equal freedom and is instituted by popular consent."[17] Accordingly, we turn now to the framers and their posture toward democracy and to the relationship between the Declaration and the Constitution. Nowhere are these matters treated more thoughtfully than in the following words of Martin Diamond:

> With the Constitution the Americans completed the half-revolution begun in 1776 and became the first modern people fully to confront the issue of democracy. But, again, the American Revolution precisely in its revolutionary thrust was simultaneously distinctively sober. . . .
> The sobriety lies in the Founding Fathers' coolheaded and cautious acceptance of democracy. Perhaps not a single American voice was raised in unqualified, doctrinaire praise of democracy. On the contrary, there was universal recognition of the problematic character of democracy, a concern for its weaknesses and a fear of its dangers. The debate in American life during the founding decade gradually became a debate over how to create a decent democratic regime. Contrary to our too complacent modern perspective regard-

---

[16] February 8, 1825, in Gaillard Hunt, ed., *The Writings of James Madison*, vol. 9 (New York: G. P. Putnam's Sons, 1900), pp. 218-219.

[17] Martin Diamond, "The Declaration and the Constitution," p. 50.

ing democracy, which assumes that a government cannot be decent unless democratic, our Founding Fathers more skeptically, sensibly, and soberly were concerned how to make this new government *decent even though democratic*. All the American revolutionaries, whether they were partisans of the theory that democratic republics had to be small or agrarian or only loosely confederated in order to remain free, or whether they retained the traditional idea that democracy had to be counterbalanced by nobility or wealth, or whether they subscribed to the large-republic theory implicit in the new Constitution—all the American revolutionaries knew that democracy was a problem in need of constant solution, in constant need of moderation, in constant need of institutions and measures to mitigate its defects and guard against its dangers.[18]

The framers, at one with the great tradition of political philosophy, viewed every form of government as problematic, as having its own peculiar liability to deterioration. Their concern was the possible corruptions of the form of government they were contemplating—the democratic form—and they spoke frankly of democracy's defects and undesirable propensities.[19] Statements like that of Edmund Randolph appear at the federal convention, that the "general object was to provide a cure for the evils under which the U.S. had laboured; that in tracing these evils to their origin every man had found it in the turbulence and follies of democracy: that some check therefore was to be sought for agst. this tendency in our Governments." Elbridge Gerry similarly noted that "the evils we experience flow from the excess of democracy. The people do not want virtue; but are the dupes of pretended patriots. . . . He had been too republican heretofore: he was still however republican, but had been taught by experience the danger of the levelling spirit."[20] These statements have been understood as a rejection of democracy itself; in fact, they were occasioned by a discussion of the composition of the House of Representatives. When the discussion is read as a whole, it becomes clear that the delegates were talking about the constitution of a legislative body *within a democratic government*. The very intensity of the concern about the dangers of the democratic form demonstrates that the framers were determined both to be democratic and to avoid the classic problems of democracies.

---

[18] Martin Diamond, "The Revolution of Sober Expectations," pp. 38-39.

[19] Martin Diamond, "The Declaration and the Constitution," p. 51.

[20] Max Farrand, ed., *Records of the Federal Convention*, vol. 1 (New Haven: Yale University Press, 1911), pp. 48-51 [May 31].

The Problem of Majority Faction

The great problem of democracies had been majority faction, or, as it has come to be known (largely due to the influence of Tocqueville and John Stuart Mill), majority tyranny. Not only did history teach that democracies inevitably degenerate into mob rule; it also taught that the tyranny of the majority was worse than other tyrannies. Edmund Burke has a superb description of the meaning of this democratic possibility:

> In a democracy the majority of the citizens is capable of exercizing the most cruel oppressions upon the minority, whenever strong divisions prevail in that kind of polity, as often they must, and that oppression of the minority will extend to far greater numbers and will be carried on with much greater fury, than can almost ever be apprehended from the dominion of a single sceptre.... Under a cruel prince they have the balmy compassion of mankind to assuage the smart of their wounds and they have the plaudits of the people to animate their generous constancy under their sufferings; but those who are subjected to wrong under multitudes are deprived of all external consolation; they seem deserted by mankind, overpowered by a conspiracy of their whole species.[21]

In *Federalist* No. 10, Madison offers his solution to the problem of majority faction, and, in *Federalist* No. 51, he argues the necessity of "auxiliary precautions" as part of that solution. Both papers rest on the sure but vulgar base of self-interest. These essays were intended by Madison to be complementary parts of a single, coherent argument; but, as it turned out, *Federalist* No. 51 proved to be peculiarly objectionable to one group of critics, the ultrademocrats, and *Federalist* No. 10 has come to repel a very different group of critics, the lukewarm democrats. To the extreme democrat, the auxiliary precautions described in *Federalist* No. 51 are certain evidence of the founders' rejection of democracy. These arrangements, including separation of powers, checks, balances, the electoral college, and even federalism, are thought to be clearly antidemocratic means for preventing the majority from ruling. On the other hand, those skeptical about democracy as such are repelled by the liberation of self-interest, especially economic self-interest, in *Federalist* No. 10. Madison's possible response to these two groups will come to light, if we ex-

---

[21] "Reflections on the Revolution in France," in *Writings and Speeches of Edmund Burke* (Boston: Little, Brown, 1901), vol. 3, pp. 397–398.

amine more carefully the relationship of self-interest and democracy in the work of the founders.

Madison's solution and the constitutional order derive from a view of human nature that has a good deal more in common with the ancient view than with the post-utopian socialist view. The American theory of human nature denies the perfectibility of man, recognizes the primary role of self-interest in human behavior, and derives from the universality of human passions (possessed equally by all men, regardless of capacity), a profound argument for equal entitlement to rights in civil society. Diamond points out that a consequence of this "debunking" view of human nature is a new and more persuasive case for democracy as such. He finds that this realistic view of man is even more devastating to the "claims or pretensions of the few than it is of the many."[22]

The founders believed that, for the first time, they had the means to render democracy safe; theirs was the "new science of politics." Madison's claim in *Federalist* No. 10—

[t]o secure the public good and private rights against the danger of [majority] faction, and at the same time to preserve the spirit and the form of popular government, is then the great object to which our inquiries are directed. . . . [I]t is the great desideratum by which alone this form of government can be rescued from the opprobrium under which it has so long labored and be recommended to the esteem and adoption of mankind

—should not be taken lightly. Coupled with a longstanding awareness of democracy's dangerous propensities was a new belief in the "capacity of mankind for self-government."

The "new science of politics," based on a debunking view of human nature, used an arrangement of institutions to create stable, decent democratic government and to free a vast part of human existence from government control. This was to be a government of limited objects or purposes, because the founding generation still understood that great governmental power—even democratic governmental power—is *always* dangerous to liberty and that liberty was the appropriate end of all government. But, as Madison explained in *Federalist* No. 10, "when a majority is included in a faction, the form of popular government, . . . enables it to sacrifice to its ruling passion or interest both the public good and the rights of other citizens." Here is no equivocation, we note, about the power of the

---

[22] "The American Idea of Equality: The View from the Founding," *Review of Politics* (July 1976), pp. 321-322.

majority. When a persistent and unified majority forms, Madison said, the institutions of government (all those devices that allegedly hamstring the democratic will) mesh gears and purr smoothly toward the goal of the majority, no matter how foolish or venal it may be. An arrangement of government institutions will not be sufficient to avert abuse of power unless a way can be found simultaneously to neutralize *the* democratic problem, majority faction.

The Principle of Representation

We have Madison's answer to this problem in the tenth *Federalist*—rich and complex, our foremost political writing. The prerequisite for his solution is the principle of representation, which makes possible extent of sphere, embracing a "great variety of interests, parties, and sects." Madison's democratic remedy for the defects of democratic government is a very large republic. He theorized that the sheer number and variety of groupings would prevent any single one from dominating national politics to the detriment of the whole. In order for a majority to form, a necessary coalescing process would occur, moderating "these majorities so that free and competent government would result democratically from them."[23]

Madison recognized that there were sources of interests and parties that could be almost fatal to this process. Among them are religious conflict (where the number of contending religions is small, perhaps as few as two, and where there is a connection between civil and religious authority) and conflict between the few rich and the many poor. Accordingly, his solution seeks to suppress these great and traditional sources of conflict and to replace them with the comparatively harmless economic conflict that results when "acquisitiveness" is "liberated" in a modern commercial setting. Economic competition among different "kinds of property," instead of primarily between rich and poor and their *amounts* of property, would be characteristic of modern society in a large diverse republic. The variety of property made possible by size is crucial to the success of the constitutional system. As Madison writes in another place, "Divide et impera, the reprobated axiom of tyranny, is under certain qualifications, the only policy, by which a republic can be administered on just principles."[24] He explained in a letter to Jefferson that

---

[23] Diamond et al., *The Democratic Republic*, p. 91.

[24] Letter to Jefferson, October 24, 1787, in Hunt, *Writings of Madison*, vol. 5, p. 31. This extraordinary letter is Madison's account to Jefferson of the work of the convention and the principles of the proposed political system.

in a republican government, "where the majority must ultimately decide," a majority cannot be prevented from oppressing the minority, unless the sphere is so enlarged that

> no common interest or passion will be likely to unite a majority of the whole number in an unjust pursuit. In a large Society, the people are broken into so many interests and parties, that a common sentiment is less likely to be felt, and the requisite concert less likely to be formed, by a majority of the whole.

The same security is necessary for the religious as well as the civil rights of individuals.

The crucial elements of Madison's system are representation, which makes possible a large republic, and a modern commercial system along the lines suggested by the writings of Adam Smith. Mr. Justice Holmes to the contrary notwithstanding, the American Constitution is not neutral with regard to economic philosophies—a point that cannot be overemphasized in an age when even enthusiastic proponents of commerce wish to forget this essential relationship. American democratic stability, decency, and liberty rest on the foundation of relatively unfettered private commerce and on the tireless struggle among individuals for their own material improvement.

We must be clear about what Madison said in *Federalist* No. 10. He was *not* narrowly and obsessively concerned with the dangers to democratic government arising from "poor" majorities. He was also troubled by, and sought to fragment, majorities united by attachment to a particular religion, to a philosophical point of view, or to a spellbinding demagogue. Madison's system has thus prevented the formation of conservative religious majorities or majorities behind such figures as Huey Long and George Wallace just as effectively as it has prevented the formation of a unified "proletariat." And, Madison wrote, the first object of government is not to protect property as such; it is to protect the diversity in the faculties of men giving rise to the differing degrees and kinds of property upon which the system relies. The protection of:

> The *diversity* in the faculties of men, from which the rights of property originate, . . . is the *first object* of government. From the protection of different and unequal faculties of acquiring property, the possession of different degrees and kinds of property immediately results; and from the influence of these on the sentiments and views of the respective proprietors ensues a division of the society into different interests and parties. [Emphasis added.]

29

Madison goes on: "The regulation of these various and interfering interests forms the principal task of modern legislation and involves the spirit of party and faction in the necessary and ordinary operations of government." Note that Madison presented a radically modern (in contrast to the ancient) view of the legitimate role of government; it is sharply limited. He insisted, however, that regulation—perhaps even what we call today trust busting—is necessary to preserve and encourage the preconditions for decent democracy; this is not laissez-faire economic thinking. Government action is necessary to keep the system open and available to the largest possible number of participants, for only wide participation in the economic system can produce the desired results. Great and permanent concentrations of wealth at the top of the population, as well as concentrations of poverty at the bottom, are equally subversive of Madison's purpose. Self-interest is the impetus, and fragmentation of tyrannical majorities is the consequence, of the successful working out of the human energies thus set in motion.

Yet surely the "auxiliary precautions" or institutional arrangements considered by Madison in *Federalist* No. 51 are evidence that the framers designed a constitution with at least some nondemocratic elements. (I hesitate to use the word *aristocratic*, so convinced am I that nothing approaching a real aristocracy—privilege inherited through birth—can be found in America.) Surely the American Constitution is a mixed one; what about separation of powers? Yet Hamilton claimed in *Federalist* No. 9 that separation of powers is part of the "new science of politics": "the regular distribution of power into distinct departments." Two points can be made here; first, separation of powers, although frequently confused with mixed regime or balanced government, is neither. Second, as a device, it is only efficacious in a wholly democratic society.

Separation of Powers

Balanced government or mixed regime is an arrangement in which governing power is divided between the few rich and the many poor (as described by Aristotle) or among the three estates or orders in society: the royalty, the nobility, and the commons. It was believed that in this way no one part of society could tyrannize over the others and, in the ancient case, that each part could realize at least partially the conception of justice appropriate to it. Crucial to a proper understanding of separation of powers, is the necessity that these orders or classes must exist in some fixed way in society; if they do not preexist, they cannot be invented for the purposes of such an arrangement.

In other words, only a political community that consisted of these three classes could have a mixed regime or balanced government. This point, which seems painfully obvious, nevertheless needs to be emphasized. America lacked the necessary requisites for mixed government —the elements to mix. The same holds true for a mixture of rich and poor. In a society where these classes are fixed, as in ancient Greece, a mixed government was possible. In a society where, by definition, these are fluid groupings, with the majority of the population tending toward a middle economic "class," there is no basis for such an arrangement.[25]

The confusion about separation of powers became apparent almost immediately upon its formal introduction into the American constitutional order and can be found in both John Adams and Thomas Jefferson.[26] Adams never quite disentangled separation of powers from balanced government in his own thinking, and, according to one scholar, tried to "define republicanism so as to accommodate the balance of the English constitution without 'either an hereditary king or an hereditary nobility.'"[27]

The necessarily democratic character of separation of powers is compellingly argued by Diamond; two of his points are indispensable here. First, "democracy is the precondition for the successful operation or working" of the device; second, "the separation of powers is intelligible only if conceived as aiming at the amelioration of modern democracy; that is, the separation has as its purpose the improvement of democracy in particular and not of government in general."[28] His argument can only be suggested here. It is that this arrangement aims at individual liberty and at limiting politics and government to "general and equal laws and their fair execution." These are peculiarly democratic problems and democratic goals.

How does the arrangement work? The powers of government are divided according to the theory of their function and placed in

---

[25] Madison shed interesting light on this in 1792, when he spoke of parties and a difference of interests and how to combat the excesses of the same. One means was "by the silent operation of laws, which, without violating the rights of property, reduce extreme wealth towards a state of mediocrity, and raise extreme indigence towards a state of comfort." He characterized this point (and the others he makes) as the language of republicanism. Hunt, *Writings of Madison*, vol. 6, p. 86.

[26] For a detailed presentation of these views, see Martin Diamond, "The Separation of Powers and the Mixed Regime," and Ann Stuart Diamond, "The Zenith of Separation of Powers Theory: The Federal Convention of 1787," in *Publius* (summer 1978).

[27] Bernard Bailyn, *The Ideological Origins of the American Revolution* (Cambridge, Mass.: Belknap Press, 1967), pp. 282, 283, fn. 50.

[28] Diamond, "Separation of Powers," pp. 39ff.

that branch where they can be most appropriately exercised—law-making powers in a legislative branch, etc. The success of the arrangement depends, Madison explained in *Federalist* No. 51, on "giving to those who administer each department the necessary constitutional means and personal motives to resist encroachment of the others." "Ambition must be made to counter ambition. The interest of the man must be connected with the constitutional rights of the place." Office-holders will tend to identify their own self-interest with the integrity of their office; this will incline them toward opposing extreme and foolish measures much of the time. The cause of liberty is served by the great difficulty that three separated branches would find in any effort to unite to oppress the populace. Here again, self-interest and jealous guarding of the powers of one's own office play the vital role.

These concepts are connected to the vital understanding that separation of powers will work only in a democracy. Diamond demonstrates this by showing that separation of powers could not produce the desired effects under certain conditions: where there is a "powerful, distinct, permanent interest in society, adverse to the rights and interests of all the others," and where family interests, profound religious divisions, or fixed oligarchical classes dominate society.[29] If a disciplined ideological party, for example, came to have dominant political power, the commitment to ideology would overrule the necessary attachment to the peculiar interests of one's office and its responsibilities and duties, upon which separation of powers depends. Instead, "these disciplined ideologues would function as a unified force thereby rendering the separation nugatory." Diamond further argues that the shared interests and perspectives of family, religion, or oligarchy would serve equally to destroy the separation; that is, these attachments would take precedence. The arrangement of separation of powers presupposes instead Madison's "heterogeneous modern large-scale representative democracy."

If separation of powers is a wholly democratic institutional device, what in the Constitution is *non*democratic, either in intention or in its operation or effect? The answer to the question depends on our perspective on democracy (the perspective common today is described at the beginning of this essay). Is it nondemocratic to slow down and moderate the will of the majority? Why? Should we take seriously the radical democratic critique of an allegedly nondemocratic constitution, that regards arrangements to produce decency and liberty *as undemocratic*? This amounts to saying that the only democratic constitutions are those that produce, by means of instant majority

---

[29] Ibid., especially pp. 40-41.

action, foolish, even tyrannical policies. Were this so, no reasonable man could actually prefer democracy—not even the ultrademocratic critics of the Constitution.

Similar misgivings apply to the critique of the Constitution by those lukewarm toward democracy. Their analysis rests on the view that indeed no thoughtful person could prefer democracy, because democracy cannot be the home of moderation or liberty. Therefore, devices to secure moderation or liberty must, by definition, be nondemocratic. This is why we must, in conclusion, ask the question, *Why* be democratic? and try to give the founders' answer to that question.

The Realization of Liberty

I have argued here, following Martin Diamond, that the Declaration of Independence is not a democratic manifesto betrayed by a conservative or reactionary Constitution. The Declaration is the nonpareil expression of the legitimate end of modern government, liberty. The Constitution is the realization of that liberty by means of the democratic form of government. The framers completed the work of the Revolution by establishing a wholly democratic—decent even though democratic—government. The stability and decency of this Constitution rest on a theory of human nature in which the role of self-interest is primary and on economic behavior generated by that self-interest. The primary protection for liberty, in all its aspects, lies in this behavior and in the constitutional institutions themselves, not in the first ten amendments, known as the Bill of Rights. Madison's profound understanding of this and its explication belong to another place, but the absence of a bill of rights may not be used as evidence that the Constitution is undemocratic by intention.[30]

But what of the electoral college? Critics from both perspectives seem to agree on the nondemocratic intentions of the framers here. A careful examination of the debates at the federal convention, however, supports a different conclusion. In the Virginia Plan, introduced at the beginning of the convention proceedings, the executive was to be chosen by the national legislature. A week later, James Wilson of Pennsylvania proposed the basic arrangement that became the electoral college, although it was first decisively rejected. After that, only

---

[30] Obviously, more needs to be said on this point. This observation refers to years of work on this problem and on Madison's central role. I can make two points briefly. First, Madison would have agreed with Hamilton's explanation of the absence of a bill of rights in *Federalist* No. 84: second, the history, at least of the First Amendment, proves that they were both right.

one significant change was made—in the event of no candidate's receiving a majority of electoral college votes, the run-off election is to be held in the House of Representatives, not the Senate.

Wilson made his proposal because he wished to see the choice of the executive made "by the people at large" without the intervention either of the states or the national legislature, so that this "mode would produce more confidence among the people in the first magistrate," particularly as a check on the national legislature.[31] Madison also believed that "the people at large was in his opinion the fittest in itself" to choose the executive. He agreed with Wilson and Gouverneur Morris that "the people generally could only know and vote for some Citizen whose merits had rendered him an object of general attention and esteem."[32] This statement was in answer to those who did not believe that the people at large could be expected to choose men of distinction and merit for the office. These critics preferred that the executive be chosen by the national legislature.

Other critics, who sought to keep the state influence in the national councils, argued for choice by the state legislatures.[33] Wilson and Gouverneur Morris wanted the conditions to create an independent executive as a necessary check on the overbearing tendencies of the legislature in a representative democracy. After the Senate—Madison's great anchor of the government—was lost to equal state representation, Madison joined them along with his considerable power of rational argument.

The device of electors to make possible choice by the people was necessitated by three practical problems: the danger of cabal and intrigue in order to influence the outcome, the problem of communication (in an age when traveling from Montpelier, Virginia, to Monticello, Virginia, was a major undertaking), and the fact that suffrage was "more diffusive in the Northern than in the Southern states; and the latter could have no influence in the election on the score of the Negroes. The substitution of electors obviated this difficulty."[34]

---

[31] Farrand, *Federal Convention*, vol. 1, pp. 68, 80.

[32] Ibid., vol. 2, pp. 56-57.

[33] I disagree here with the analysis of Martin Diamond that the device of electors was "[f]irst and above all,... as a nationalizing substitute for the state legislatures." This concern surfaces with force later in the convention, but, at the time Wilson made his proposal, the crisis over the composition of the Senate and equal state representation in that body, which had so many consequences both for the convention and the subsequent frame of government, had not yet occurred. *The Electoral College and the American Idea of Democracy* (Washington, D.C.: American Enterprise Institute, 1977), p. 3.

[34] Farrand, *Federal Convention*, vol. 2, p. 57. Madison speaking.

There is no language at the federal convention suggesting that the framers expected electors to use such autonomy in choosing a president that the democratic origins of the concept would be lost. The source of that vain hope was Alexander Hamilton, writing in *Federalist* No. 68. By 1805, electors considered themselves morally bound by the popular vote, and there have been only roughly ten out of twenty thousand electoral votes cast that strayed from the popular vote.

The indispensable question then is, How democratic is the Constitution? "It is the ground on which all else rests because the question of democracy speaks to the fundamental nature of a regime. . . . The answer to the question profoundly influences both practical politics and the way politics is studied."[35] The form of government is conducive to certain forms of political and social behavior, as well as economic behavior, and suppresses other forms of behavior. It may be said that a certain kind of citizen is produced, even in modern liberal democracies, by the form of the constitution.[36] The centrality of the question is attested to by the disputed nature of the answer and the persistence of the dispute. In view of its dangerous propensities, constituting democracy was the most difficult task of founding, and democratic citizenship is the most demanding kind of citizenship. As with marriage, one has constantly to work at democracy.

If democracy is so demanding and was avoided by men for centuries because it always culminated in disaster, why did the founders prefer it? Why be democratic? The founders' reasons were not egalitarian in the "leveling" sense; that is, they were not the reasons why democracy is usually preferred today. Thomas Jefferson desired democracy because he believed it would do away with artificial distinctions and barriers to real merit; instead it would allow true merit and distinction to be realized and to have its play in the society. Today, of course, the spirit of our institutions has become antithetical to natural merit; those who believe in real differences in human capacity, and that a society that suppresses them cannot survive indefinitely, are considered "elitist" and even dangerously reactionary. Nevertheless, the elevation of natural merit was a reason why thoughtful men could and did desire democratic institutions.

The claim to rule as of right, based on birth, property, wisdom, or experience, became increasingly illegitimate. This resulted in good part from the acceptance of Locke's theories on the precivil condition

---

[35] Diamond et al., *The Democratic Republic*, p. 84.
[36] Martin Diamond, "Ethics and Politics: The American Way," in Robert Horwitz, ed., *Moral Foundations of the American Republic* (Charlottesville: University of Virginia Press, 1977).

of man, on natural rights, and on the limits of government. He taught that political communities come into being by consent, that men are perfectly equal in the state of nature, and that in return for protection against the inconveniences of that natural state, men agree to submit to a civil authority which recognizes their individual rights. All men, high and low, equally desire comfortable self-preservation.

Limited Government

Locke and others made the case for radically limiting the scope of government. The traditional ends of government—molding citizens morally or intellectually—were abandoned as utopian by liberal theorists, in favor of leaving such matters to private decisions. This profound reduction in government's legitimate objects made self-government possible. Citizen legislatures that had to pay the taxes they levied and fight the wars they declared were safest to the largest number of men and did not represent an interest (like the monarch) adverse to or independent of the body of society. They *were* the body of society. Their task was now within the capacity of any public-spirited citizen. Governing no longer required the wisdom and experience it had in the past. Government thus limited and legislatures thus subject to their own laws were believed safer to liberty than other kinds of arrangements.

In America, society was already democratic in that the possession of wealth was fluid, not fixed, and multidirectional: wide-ranging social mobility was the rule, not the exception. The framers themselves were examples of these realities and understood their meaning. George Mason observed at the federal convention

> we had been too democratic but [he] was afraid we sd. incautiously run into the opposite extreme. We ought to attend to the rights of every class of people. He had often wondered at the indifference of the superior classes of society to this dictate of humanity and policy, considering that however affluent their circumstances, or elevated their situations, might be, the course of a few years, not only might but certainly would, distribute their posterity throughout the lowest classes of Society. Every selfish motive therefore, every family attachment, ought to recommend such a system of policy as would provide no less carefully for the rights— and happiness of the lowest than of the highest orders of Citizens. [May 31]

We may then say that, along with other reasons, self-interest dictated the framers' preference for democracy. It was the only form of government that gave equal political rights to the lowest as well as to the highest order of citizens and thus made it possible for citizens to rise as high as their talents could take them. Hamilton, after all, was an illegitimate son whose success, based on extraordinary talents, was made possible by a democratic setting. John Adams did not begin life as one of the highest orders of citizens. The founding generation appreciated fully the opportunities opened by democracy for men of capacity and did not intend to foreclose them, either for themselves or for their posterity, by a constitution that restricted political power to property or birth. There are, of course, no such restrictions in the Constitution.

The final reasons for preferring democracy relate to the individual citizen. In a democracy, greater numbers of ordinary people achieve a higher level of material and psychic well-being and their claim to have the ultimate power over how they are governed cannot be denied. Democracy provides opportunities for vast numbers of citizens to participate in the political process at all levels of government; citizens come to assume responsibility for themselves and for others in a way permitted by no other form of government.

The founders intended to create, and did create, a wholly democratic Constitution. Prudently mindful of the pitfalls of democracy, they introduced a number of institutional devices to protect liberty from an immoderate majority will, while permitting moderate majority will to prevail. Civil and religious liberty are further protected by a large, diverse, commercial society, in which dangerous majorities are fragmented by the informal workings of the social and economic systems. This unusually thoughtful generation preferred democracy because it removed barriers to natural merit, because it improved the lives of the largest numbers of ordinary folk, because it allowed men to choose how they would be governed and to take responsibility for that choice, and because they believed that under a democratic constitution the country would prosper and a new age in the relations of nations would begin.[37]

Constituting democracy involved a remarkable act of faith as well as skill. The cheerful consequence of an otherwise cheerless view of human nature was the belief that men could govern themselves decently in an arrangement where liberty *and* stability could coexist. It was a leap into the unknown, an act of political courage that we

---

[37] Some framers even believed that the quality of foreign affairs would be improved and that democratic countries would engage in fewer wars. See Madison's "The Letters of Helvidius," in Hunt, *Writings of Madison*, vol. 5, pp. 138-188. See also Felix Gilbert, *The Beginnings of American Foreign Policy* (New York: Harper and Row, 1965), especially chap. 3.

cannot even imagine. No government based on the principle of self-government in a large, diverse country had ever been known. The framers stepped into the abyss, coolly confident that it would work the way they expected; they thereby rescued democratic government from the opprobrium under which it had so long labored and recommended it to the esteem and adoption of mankind. At bottom, the Constitution rested on a conviction that the people have enough democratic virtue—public-spiritedness and concern for the common good—to be trusted with their own affairs. In the words of James Madison,

> But I go on this great republican principle, that the people will have virtue and intelligence to select men of virtue and wisdom. Is there no virtue among us? If there be not, we are in a wretched situation. No theoretical checks, no form of government, can render us secure. To suppose any form of government will secure liberty or happiness without any virtue in the people, is a chimerical idea. If there be sufficient virtue and intelligence in the community, it will be exercised in the selection of these men; so that we do not depend on their virtue, or put confidence in our rulers, but in the people who are to choose them.[38]

I conclude with a personal note: All of this analysis, interpretation, and argument rests on the work of Martin Diamond, so much so that of many parts I am not sure what is his and what is mine. Yet I cannot hold him responsible for all of the implications of the essay. In particular, I would not want to have to prove that he would fully agree with my own enthusiastic and unclouded endorsement of American democracy as embodied—more than anywhere else—in the political philosophy and statesmanship of James Madison.

---

[38] June 20, 1788. Jonathan Elliot, *Debates in the Several State Conventions on the Adoption of the Federal Constitution* (Philadelphia: Lippincott, 1907). Madison's use of "virtue" here means public-spiritedness.

3

The Constitution as an Elitist Document

Michael Parenti

How democratic is the Constitution? Not as democratic as we have been taught to believe. I will argue that the intent of the framers of the Constitution was to *contain* democracy, rather than give it free rein, and dilute the democratic will, rather than mobilize it. In addition, their goal was to construct a centralized power to serve the expanding interests of the manufacturing, commercial, land-owning, and financial classes, rather than the needs of the populace. Evidence for this, it will be shown, can be found in the framers' opinions and actions and in the Constitution they fashioned. Finally, I will argue that the elitist design of the Constitution continues to function as intended, serving as a legitimating cloak and workable system for the propertied interests at the expense of the ordinary populace.

Class and Power in Early America

It is commonly taught that in the eighteenth and nineteenth centuries men of property preferred a laissez-faire government, one that kept its activities to a minimum. In actuality, they were not against a strong state but against state restrictions on business enterprise. They never desired to remove civil authority from economic affairs but to ensure that it worked *for*, rather than against, the interests of property. This meant they often had to move toward new and stronger state formations.

   Adam Smith, who is above suspicion in his dedication to classical capitalism, argued that, as wealth increased in scope, government would have to perform still greater services on behalf of the propertied class. "The necessity of civil government," he wrote, "grows up with the acquisition of valuable property."[1] More importantly, Smith argued seventy years before Marx, "Civil authority, so far as it is instituted for the security of property, is in reality instituted for the defense of the rich against the poor, or of those who have some property against those who have none at all."[2]

Smith's views of the purposes of government were shared by the rich and the wellborn who lived in America during the period between the Revolution and the framing of the Constitution. Rather than keeping their distance from government, they set the dominant political tone.

> Their power was born of place, position, and fortune. They were located at or near the seats of government and they were in direct contact with legislatures and government officers. They influenced and often dominated the local newspapers which voiced the ideas and interests of commerce and identified them with the good of the whole people, the state, and the nation. The published writings of the leaders of the period are almost without exception those of merchants, of their lawyers, or of politicians sympathetic with them.[3]

The United States of 1787 has been described as an "egalitarian" society free from the extremes of want and wealth which characterized the Old World, but there were landed estates and colonial mansions that bespoke an impressive munificence. From the earliest English settlements, men of influence had received vast land grants from the crown. By 1700, three-fourths of the acreage in New York belonged to fewer than a dozen persons. In the interior of Virginia, seven persons owned a total of 1,732,000 acres.[4] By 1760, fewer than 500 men in five colonial cities controlled most of the commerce, banking, mining, and manufacturing on the eastern seaboard and owned much of the land.[5]

Here and there could be found farmers, shop owners, and tradesmen who, by the standards of the day, might be judged as comfortably situated. The bulk of the agrarian population were poor freeholders, tenants, squatters, and indentured and hired hands. The cities also had their poor—cobblers, weavers, bakers, blacksmiths,

---

[1] Adam Smith, *An Inquiry into the Nature and Causes of the Wealth of Nations* (Chicago: Encyclopaedia Britannica, Inc., 1952), p. 309.

[2] Ibid., p. 311.

[3] Merrill Jensen, *The New Nation* (New York: Random House, 1950), p. 178.

[4] Sidney H. Aronson, *Status and Kinship in the Higher Civil Service* (Cambridge, Mass.: Harvard University Press, 1964), p. 35.

[5] Ibid., p. 41.

peddlers, laborers, clerks, and domestics, who worked long hours for meager sums.[6]

As of 1787, property qualifications left perhaps more than a third of the white male population disfranchised.[7] Property qualifications for holding office were so steep as to prevent most voters from qualifying as candidates. Thus, a member of the New Jersey legislature had to be worth at least 1,000 pounds, while state senators in South Carolina were required to possess estates worth at least 7,000 pounds, clear of debt.[8] In addition, the practice of oral voting, the lack of a secret ballot, and an "absence of a real choice among candidates and programs" led to "widespread apathy."[9] As a result, men of substance monopolized the important offices. "Who do they represent?" Josiah Quincy asked of the South Carolina legislature. "The laborer, the mechanic, the tradesman, the farmer, the husbandman or yeoman? No, the representatives are almost if not wholly rich planters."[10]

Dealing with Insurgency

The Constitution was framed by financially successful planters, merchants, lawyers, and creditors, many linked by kinship and marriage and by years of service in Congress, the military, or diplomatic service. They congregated in Philadelphia in 1787 for the professed purpose of revising the Articles of Confederation and strengthening the powers of the central government. They were impelled by a desire to do something about the increasingly insurgent spirit evidenced among poorer people. Fearful of losing control of their state governments, the framers looked to a national government as a means of

---

[6] Ibid., passim.

[7] This is Beard's estimate regarding New York. Charles A. Beard, *An Economic Interpretation of the Constitution of the United States* (New York: Macmillan, 1936), pp. 67-68. In a few states like Pennsylvania and Georgia, suffrage was more widespread; in others it was even more restricted than New York; see Arthur Ekrich, Jr., *The American Democratic Tradition* (New York: Macmillan, 1963). For a pioneer work on this subject, see A. E. McKinley, *The Suffrage Franchise in the Thirteen English Colonies in America* (Philadelphia: B. Franklin, 1969, originally published 1905). Robert E. Brown makes the argument that Massachusetts was close to being both an economic and political democracy— which would have been alarming news to the Boston aristocracy of manufacturers, merchants, and large property holders. He conjectures that property requirements of a 40 shilling freehold could be easily met and that rural underrepresentation (during the same period that produced Shays' Rebellion) was due more to indifference than to disfranchisement. See his *Middle-Class Democracy and the Revolution in Massachusetts* (Ithaca, N.Y.: Cornell University Press, 1955).

[8] Beard, *An Economic Interpretation*, pp. 68, 70.

[9] Aronson, *Status and Kinship*, p. 49.

[10] Ibid., p. 49.

protecting their interests. Even in a state like South Carolina, where the propertied class was distinguished by the intensity of its desire to avoid any strong federation, the rich and the well-born, once faced with the possibility of rule by the common people "and realizing that a political alliance with conservatives from other states would be a safeguard if the radicals should capture the state government . . . gave up 'state rights' for 'nationalism' without hestitation."[11] It swiftly became their view that a central government would be less accessible to the populace and would be better able to provide the protections and services that their class so needed.

The landed, manufacturing, and merchant interests needed a central government that would provide a stable currency; impose uniform standards for trade; tax directly; regulate commerce; improve roads, canals, and harbors; provide protection against foreign imports and against the discrimination suffered by American shipping; and provide a national force to subjugate the Indians and secure the value of western lands. They needed a government that would honor at face value the huge sums of public securities they held and would protect them from paper-money schemes and from the large debtor class, the land-hungry agrarians, and the growing numbers of urban poor.

The nationalist conviction that arose so swiftly among men of property during the 1780s was not the product of a strange transcendent inspiration; it was not a "dream of nation-building" that suddenly possessed them as might a collective religious experience. (If so, they were remarkably successful in keeping it a secret in their public and private communications.) Rather, their newly acquired nationalism was a practical and urgent response to material conditions affecting them in a most immediate way. Gorham of Massachusetts, Hamilton of New York, Morris of Pennsylvania, Washington of Virginia, and Pinckney of South Carolina had a greater identity of interest with each other than with debt-burdened neighbors in their home counties. Their like-minded commitment to a central government was born of a common class interest stronger than state boundaries.

The rebellious populace of that day has been portrayed as irresponsible and parochial spendthrifts who never paid their debts and who believed in nothing more than timid state governments and inflated paper money. Little is said by most scholars of the period (including contributors to this volume) about the actual plight of the common people, the great bulk of whom lived at a subsistence level. Farm tenants were burdened by heavy rents and hard labor. Small

---

[11] Merrill Jensen, *The Articles of Confederation* (Madison: University of Wisconsin Press, 1948), p. 30.

farmers were hurt by the low prices merchants offered for their crops and by the high costs for merchandised goods. They often bought land at inflated prices, only to see its value collapse and to find themselves unable to meet their mortgage obligations. Their labor and their crops usually were theirs in name only. To survive, they frequently had to borrow money at high interest rates. To meet their debts, they mortgaged their future crops and went still deeper into debt. Large numbers were caught in that cycle of rural indebtedness which is the common fate of agrarian peoples in many countries to this day. The artisans, small tradesmen, and workers (or "mechanics," as they were called) in the towns were not much better off, being "dependent on the wealthy merchants who ruled them economically and socially."[12]

During the 1780s, the jails were crowded with debtors. Among the people, there grew the feeling that the revolution against England had been fought for naught. Angry, armed crowds in several states began blocking foreclosures and sales of seized property, and opening up jails. They gathered at county towns to prevent the courts from presiding over debtor cases. In the winter of 1787, farmers in western Massachusetts led by Daniel Shays took up arms. But their rebellion was forcibly put down by the state militia after some ragged skirmishes.[13]

Containing the Spread of Democracy

The specter of Shays' Rebellion hovered over the delegates who gathered in Philadelphia three months later, confirming their worst fears about the populace. They were determined that persons of birth and fortune should control the affairs of the nation and check the "leveling impulses" of that propertyless multitude which composed "the majority faction." "To secure the public good and private rights against the danger of such a faction," wrote James Madison in *Federalist* No. 10, "and at the same time preserve the spirit and form of popular government is then the great object to which our inquiries are directed." Here Madison touched the heart of the matter: how to keep the *spirit* and *form* of popular government with only a minimum

---

[12] Ibid., pp. 9-10. "In addition to being frequently in debt for their lands," Beard noted, "the small farmers were dependent upon the towns for most of the capital to develop their resources. They were, in other words, a large debtor class, to which must be added, of course, the urban dwellers who were in a like unfortunate condition." Beard, *An Economic Interpretation*, p. 28.

[13] For a study of this incident, see Monroe Stearns, *Shays' Rebellion, 1786-7: Americans Take Up Arms Against Unjust Laws* (New York: Franklin Watts, 1968).

of the *substance*, how to provide the appearance of republicanism without suffering its leveling effects, how to construct a government that would win mass acquiescence but would not tamper with the existing class structure, a government strong enough both to service the growing needs of an entrepreneurial class while withstanding the egalitarian demands of the poor and propertyless.

The framers of the Constitution could agree with Madison when he wrote in the same *Federalist* No. 10 that "the most common and durable source of factions has been the various and unequal distribution of property. Those who hold and those who are without property have ever formed distinct interests in society." They were of the opinion that democracy was "the worst of all political evils," as Elbridge Gerry put it. Both he and Madison warned of "the danger of the leveling spirit." "The people," said Roger Sherman, "should have as little to do as may be about the Government." And according to Alexander Hamilton, "All communities divide themselves into the few and the many. The first are the rich and the well-born, the other the mass of the people. . . . The people are turbulent and changing; they seldom judge or determine right."[14]

The delegates spent many weeks debating their interests, but these were the differences of merchants, slave owners, and manufacturers, a debate of haves versus haves in which each group sought safeguards within the new Constitution for its particular concerns. Added to this were the inevitable disagreements that arise over the best means of achieving agreed-upon ends. Questions of structure and authority occupied a good deal of the delegates' time: How much representation should the large and small states have? How might the legislature be organized? How should the executive be selected? What length of tenure should exist for the different officeholders? *Yet, questions of enormous significance, relating to the new government's ability to protect the interests of property, were agreed upon with surprisingly little debate.* For on these issues, there were no dirt farmers or poor artisans attending the convention to proffer an opposing viewpoint. The debate between haves and have-nots never occurred.

The portions of the Constitution giving the federal government the power to support commerce and protect property were decided

---

[14] The quotations by Gerry, Madison, Sherman, and Hamilton are taken from Max Farrand, ed., *Records of the Federal Convention* (New Haven: Yale University Press, 1927), vol. 1, passim. For further testimony by the Founding Fathers and other early leaders, see John C. Miller, *Origins of the American Revolution* (Boston: Little, Brown, 1943), pp. 491 ff. and Andrew C. McLaughlin, *A Constitutional History of the United States* (New York: Appleton-Century, 1935), pp. 141-144.

upon after amiable deliberation and with remarkable dispatch considering their importance. Thus all of Article I, Section 8 was adopted within a few days.[15] This section gave to Congress the powers needed by the propertied class for the expansion of its commerce, trade, and industry, specifically the authority to (1) regulate commerce among the states and with foreign nations and Indian tribes, (2) lay and collect taxes and impose duties and tariffs on imports but not on commercial exports, (3) establish a national currency and regulate its value, (4) "borrow Money on the credit of the United States"—a measure of special interest to creditors,[16] (5) fix the standard of weights and measures necessary for trade, (6) protect the value of securities and currency against counterfeiting, (7) establish "uniform Laws on the subject of Bankruptcies throughout the United States," and (8) "pay the Debts and provide for the common Defense and general Welfare of the United States."

Some of the delegates were land speculators who expressed a concern about western holdings; accordingly, Congress was given the "Power to dispose of and make all needful Rules and Regulations respecting the Territory or other Property belong to the United States. . . ." Some delegates speculated in highly inflated and nearly worthless Confederation securities. Under Article VI, all debts incurred by the confederation were valid against the new government, a provision that allowed speculators to make generous profits when their securities were honored at face value.[17]

[15] John Bach McMaster, "Framing the Constitution," in his *The Political Depravity of the Founding Fathers* (New York: Farrar, Straus, 1964, originally published in 1896), p. 137. Farrand refers to the consensus for a strong national government that emerged after the small states had been given equal representation in the Senate. Much of the work that followed "was purely formal" albeit sometimes time-consuming. See Max Farrand, *The Framing of the Constitution of the United States* (New Haven: Yale University Press, 1913), pp. 134-135.

[16] The original wording was "borrow money and emit bills." The latter phrase was deleted after Gouverneur Morris warned that "the Monied interest" would oppose the Constitution if paper notes were not prohibited. There was much strong feeling about this among creditors. In any case, it was assumed that the borrowing power would allow for "safe and proper" public notes should they be necessary. See Farrand, *The Framing of the Constitution*, p. 147.

[17] See Beard, *An Economic Interpretation*, passim. The profits accrued to holders of public securities were in the millions. On the question of speculation in western lands, Hugh Williamson, a North Carolina delegate, wrote to Madison a year after the convention: "For myself, I conceive that my opinions are not biassed by private Interests, but having claims to a considerable Quantity of Land in the Western Country, I am fully persuaded that the Value of those Lands must be increased by an efficient federal Government." Ibid., p. 50. Critiques of Beard have been made by Robert E. Brown, *Charles Beard and the American Constitution* (Princeton, N.J.: Princeton University Press, 1956) and Forrest McDonald, *We the People—The Economic Origins of the Constitution* (Chicago: Chicago University Press, 1958).

In the interest of merchants and creditors, the states were prohibited from issuing paper money or imposing duties on imports and exports or interfering with the payment of debts by passing any "Law impairing the Obligation of Contracts." The Constitution guaranteed "Full Faith and Credit" in each state "to the Acts, Records, and judicial Proceedings" of other states, thus allowing creditors to pursue their debtors more effectively.

The property interests of slave owners were looked after. To give the slave-owning states a greater influence, three-fifths of the slave population were to be counted when calculating the representation deserved by each state in the lower house. The importation of slaves was allowed until 1808. Under Article IV, slaves who escaped from one state to another had to be delivered to the original owner upon claim, a provision unanimously adopted at the convention.

The framers believed the states acted with insufficient force against popular uprisings, so Congress was given the task of "organizing, arming, and disciplining the Militia" and calling it forth, among other reasons, to "suppress Insurrections." The federal government was empowered to protect the states "against domestic Violence." Provision was made for "the Erection of Forts, Magazines, Arsenals, dock-Yards and other needful Buildings" and for the maintenance of an army and navy for both national defense and to establish an armed federal presence within the potentially insurrectionary states—a provision that was to prove a godsend a century later when the army was used repeatedly to break strikes by miners, railroad employees, and factory workers.

In keeping with their desire to contain the majority, the founders inserted "auxiliary precautions" *designed to fragment power without democratizing it.* By separating the executive, legislative, and judiciary functions and then providing a system of checks and balances among the various branches, including staggered elections, executive veto, Senate confirmation of appointments and ratification of treaties, and a bicameral legislature, they hoped to dilute the impact of popular sentiments. They also contrived an elaborate and difficult process for amending the Constitution. *To the extent that it existed at all, the majoritarian principle was tightly locked into a system of minority vetoes, making sweeping popular actions nearly impossible.*

The propertyless majority, as Madison pointed out in *Federalist* No. 10, must not be allowed to concert in common cause against the established economic order.[18] First, it was necessary to prevent unity

---

[18] *Federalist* No. 10 can be found in any of the good editions of *The Federalist Papers.* It is one of the most significant essays on American politics ever written. With clarity and economy of language, it explains, as do few other short works,

of public sentiment by enlarging the polity and then compartmental-izing it into geographically insulated political communities. The larger the nation, the greater the "variety of parties and interests" and the more difficult it would be for a majority to find itself and act in unison. As Madison argued, "A rage for paper money, for an abolition of debts, for an equal division of property, or for any other wicked project will be less apt to pervade the whole body of the Union than a particular member of it. . . ." An uprising of impoverished farmers could threaten Massachusetts at one time and Rhode Island at another, but a national government would be large and varied enough to contain each of these and insulate the rest of the nation from the contamination of rebellion.

Political Diversity

Contemporary political scientists have said different things about the concept of political diversity. Some presume that a wide variety of interests produces moderation and compromise, it being argued that the "cross-pressured" lawmaker and voter and the multigroup polity are more likely to avoid the "extremist" solutions that are presumed to inflict those possessed of a single-minded, homogeneous political interest. In contrast, Madison welcomed diversity because it would produce not compromise but division. It would keep the mass of people divided against each other, unable to concert against the opulent class.

    Political scientists have also feared that too great a multiplicity of interests makes compromise impossible, leading to the kind of factionalism and instability that supposedly result when a vast array of irreconcilable demands are made on the polity. Here too, Madison was of a different mind. For him, the danger was centripetal, not centrifugal. The problem was not factionalism, as such, but democ-racy. His concern was that the people might *not* be riddled with divisions, that they might unify in common cause as an oppressive majority "faction."

    Here I would enter a qualification. A close reading of *Federalist* No. 10 actually uncovers two themes. The first is the one just men-tioned, the one that occupied Madison's thoughts before and during the convention: the relation between the propertyless and the prop-

how a government may utilize the republican principle to contain the populace and protect the propertied few from the propertyless many. It confronts, if not solves, the essential question of how government may reconcile the tensions between liberty, authority, and dominant class interest. In effect, the Tenth *Federalist* Paper maps out a method, relevant to this day, of preserving the existing undemocratic class structure under the legitimizing cloak of democratic forms.

ertied, the division that was "the most common and durable source of factions," factions which "ever formed distinct interests in society." But in the same paragraph of that same great essay, Madison introduced another theme, shifting the focus from the divisions between the propertied and the propertyless to the divisions *among* the propertied. "A landed interest, a manufacturing interest, a mercantile interest, a moneyed interest grow up of necessity in civilized nations. . . ." For all his supposed concern for "factions," Madison was not too worried about *these* factions. Unlike the factionalism between the propertied and propertyless that necessitated the whole great effort in Philadelphia and the need for a central government, the minority factions of propertied interests caused him no alarm.[19]

True, these minority factions might occasionally be a nuisance; they might "clog the administration" and even "convulse the society." But for some unstated reason, they would never be able "to sacrifice . . . the public good and the rights of other citizens," nor could any propertied faction "mask its violence under the forms of the Constitution." Only the majority faction was capable of such evils. Only the propertyless majority was capable of "improper and wicked projects" against property. The propertied interests, whatever their particular differences, would never advocate "an abolition of debts" or "an equal division of property"; they would never jeopardize the institution of property and wealth and the untrammeled uses thereof, which in their eyes—and Madison's—constituted the essence of "liberty."

There was, then, no need to impose constitutional checks upon the haves. If a larger polity would make it difficult for the populace to coalesce, it would do just the opposite for the propertied elites, allowing them to organize a centralized force to protect themselves from the turbulent plebeians within the various states. They would do well to settle their particular differences and work in unison to defend their common class interests. Indeed, in large part, that was

---

[19] See the fine discussion in Jerrold E. Schneider, *Ideological Coalitions in Congress* (Westport, Conn.: Greenwood Press, 1979), pp. 22-24. It is interesting to note that Madison, the Virginian, repeatedly argued against giving the small states an equal voice in the Senate with the large ones. Representation should be proportional to population, with no special protections for the less populous states. On this question, he evidenced not the slightest fear of majoritarian dominance, no difficulty in brushing aside the anxieties of the "minority" smaller states. See for instance his lengthy comments of June 28 and July 14, 1787, in Madison's *The Debates in the Federal Convention of 1787 Which Framed the Constitution of the United States of America*, ed. Gaillard Hunt and James Brown Scott (New York: Oxford University Press, 1920), pp. 177-180, 256-258. To repeat, Madison's fear was not of some abstract theoretical majority but of a particular *class* majority, a democracy.

what the Philadelphia Convention was all about. Madison wanted what every elite has ever wanted, unity of purpose within his own class and divisions and conflicts within the other, larger one.

By focusing on Madison's second theme, the diversity of supposedly self-regulating propertied interests, modern-day political scientists discovered pluralism. By ignoring his first and major theme, the conflict between haves and have-nots, they have yet to discover class conflict.

Besides preventing the people from finding *horizontal* cohesion, the Constitution was designed to dilute their *vertical* force, blunting its upward thrust upon government by interjecting indirect and staggered forms of representation. Thus, the senators from each state were to be elected by their respective state legislatures and were to have rotated terms of six years. The chief executive was to be selected by an electoral college voted by the people but, as anticipated by the framers, composed of men of substance and prominence who would gather in their various states and choose a president of their own liking. The Supreme Court was to be elected by no one, its justices being appointed to life tenure by the president and confirmed by the Senate.[20]

This system of checks would be the best safeguard against "agrarian attempts" and "symptoms of a leveling spirit," observed Madison at the convention. In those same remarks, he opposed a six-year term for the Senate, preferring a nine-year one because he believed the Senate should be composed of "a portion of enlightened citizens whose limited number and firmness might seasonably interpose against" popular impetuosity.[21] Exactly who were the "enlightened citizens"? Certainly not the tenants and squatters, nor even the average freeholder. Only the men of substance. If wealth were not a sufficient cause of enlightenment, it was almost always a necessary condition for Madison and his colleagues. Who else would have the breeding, education, and experience to govern? While often treated as an abstract virtue, "enlightened" rule had a real class meaning.

The only portion of government directly elected by the people was the House of Representatives. Many of the delegates would have preferred excluding the public entirely from direct representation. John Mercer observed that he found nothing in the proposed Constitution more objectionable than "the mode of election by the

---

[20] In time, of course, the electoral college proved to be something of a rubber stamp, and the Seventeenth Amendment, adopted in 1913, provided for the popular election of the Senate.

[21] Madison's speech of June 26, 1787, in *The Debates in the Federal Convention*, p. 167.

people. The people cannot know and judge of the characters of Candidates. The worst possible choice will be made." Others were concerned that demagogues would ride into office on a populist tide only to pillage the treasury and wreak havoc on all. "The time is not distant," warned Gouverneur Morris, "when this Country will abound with mechanics and manufacturers [industrial workers] who will receive their bread from their employers. Will such men be the secure and faithful Guardians of liberty? . . . Children do not vote. Why? Because they want prudence, because they have no will of their own. The ignorant and dependent can be as little trusted with the public interest."[22]

Several considerations softened the framers' determination to contain democracy. First and most important, the delegates recognized that there were limits to what the states would ratify. They also understood that if the federal government were to have any kind of stability, it must gain some measure of popular acceptance. Hence, for all their class biases, they were inclined to "leave something for the People," even if it were only "the *spirit* and *form* of popular government," to recall Madison's words. In addition, some delegates feared not only the tyranny of the many but the machinations of the few. It was Madison who reminded his colleagues that in protecting themselves from the multitude, they must not reintroduce a "cabal" or a monarchy, thus erring in the opposite direction.

Plotters or Patriots?

The question of whether the founders were motivated by financial or national interest has been debated since Charles Beard published *An Economic Interpretation of the Constitution* in 1913. It was Beard's view that the delegates were guided by their class interests. Arguing against Beard's thesis are those who believe that the framers were concerned with higher things than lining their purses and protecting their property. True, they were moneyed men who profited directly from policies initiated under the new Constitution, but they were motivated by a concern for nation building that went beyond their particular class interests, the argument goes.[23] To paraphrase

---

22 Farrand, *Records of the Federal Convention*, vol. 2, pp. 200 ff.

23 For some typical apologistic arguments on behalf of the "Founding Fathers," see Broadus Mitchell and Louise Pearson Mitchell, *A Biography of the Constitution of the United States* (New York: Oxford University Press, 1964), pp. 46-51, and David G. Smith, *The Convention and the Constitution* (New York: St. Martin's Press, 1965), chap. 3. Smith argues that the framers had not only economic motives but "larger" political objectives, as if the political had no relation to the economic or as if the economic interests were less selfish because they were national in financial scope.

Justice Holmes, these men invested their belief to make a nation; they did not make a nation because they had invested. "High-mindedness is not impossible to man," Holmes reminded us.

That is exactly the point: High-mindedness is one of man's most common attributes even when, or especially when, he is pursuing his personal and class interest. The fallacy is to presume that there is a dichotomy between the desire to build a strong nation and the desire to protect property and that the delegates could not have been motivated by both. In fact, like most other people, they believed that what was good for themselves was ultimately good for the entire society. Their universal values and their class interests went hand in hand; to discover the existence of the "higher" sentiment does not eliminate the self-interested one.

Most persons believe in their own virtue. The founders never doubted the nobility of their effort and its importance for the generations to come. Just as many of them could feel dedicated to the principle of "liberty for all" and at the same time own slaves, so could they serve both their nation and their estates. The point is not that they were devoid of the grander sentiments of nation building but that *there was nothing in the concept of nation which worked against their class interest and a great deal that worked for it.*

People tend to perceive things in accordance with the position they occupy in the social structure; that position is largely—although not exclusively—determined by their class status. Even if we deny that the framers were motivated by the desire for personal gain that moves others, we cannot dismiss the existence of their class interest. They may not have been solely concerned with getting their own hands in the till, although enough of them did, but they were admittedly preoccupied with defending the propertied few from the propertyless many—for the ultimate benefit of all, as they understood it. "The Constitution," as Staughton Lynd noted, "was the settlement of a revolution. What was at stake for Hamilton, Livingston, and their opponents, was more than speculative windfalls in securities; it was the question, what kind of society would emerge from the revolution when the dust had settled, and on which class the political center of gravity would come to rest."[24]

---

24 Staughton Lynd, *Class Conflict, Slavery and the United States Constitution* (Indianapolis: Bobbs-Merrill, 1967), selection in Irwin Unger, ed., *Beyond Liberalism: The New Left Views American History* (Waltham, Mass.: Xerox College Publishing, 1971), p. 17. For discussions of the class interests behind the American Revolution, see Alfred F. Young, ed., *The American Revolution: Explorations in the History of American Radicalism* (DeKalb, Ill.: Northern Illinois University Press, 1976).

The small farmers, tradesmen, and debtors who opposed a central government have been described as motivated by self-serving parochial interests—as opposed to the supposedly higher-minded statesmen who journeyed to Philadelphia and others of their class who supported ratification.[25] How or why the propertied rich became visionary nation builders is never explained. In truth, it was not their minds that were so much broader but their economic interests. Their motives were neither higher nor lower than those of any other social group struggling for place and power in the United States of 1787–1789. They pursued their material interests as single-mindedly as any small freeholder—if not more so. Possessing more time, money, information, and organization, they enjoyed superior results. How could they have acted otherwise? For them to have ignored the conditions of governance necessary for the maintenance of their enterprises would have amounted to committing class suicide—and they were not about to do that. They were a rising bourgeoisie rallying around a central power in order to advance their class interests. Some of us are quite willing to accept the existence of such a material-based nationalism in the history of other countries, but not in our own.

Finally, those who argue that the founders were motivated primarily by high-minded objectives consistently overlook the fact that the delegates repeatedly stated their intention to erect a government strong enough to protect the haves from the have-nots. They gave voice to the crassest class prejudices and never found it necessary to disguise the fact—as have latter-day apologists—that their uppermost concern was to diminish popular control and resist all tendencies toward class equalization (or "leveling," as it was called). Their opposition to democracy and their dedication to the propertied and moneyed interests were unabashedly and openly avowed. Their preoccupation was so pronounced that one delegate did finally complain of hearing too much about how the purpose of government was to protect property. He wanted it noted that the ultimate objective of government was the ennoblement of mankind—a fine sentiment that evoked no opposition from his colleagues as they continued about their business.

An Elitist Document

More important than conjecturing about the framers' motives is to look at the Constitution they fashioned, for it tells a good deal about their objectives. It was, and still is, largely an elitist document,

---

[25] See the comments in Gordon Wood's essay in this volume.

more concerned with securing property interests than personal liberties. Bills of attainder and ex post facto laws are expressly prohibited, and Article I, Section 9, assures us that "the Privilege of the Writ of Habeas Corpus shall not be suspended, unless when in Cases of Rebellion or Invasion the public Safety may require it," a restriction that leaves authorities with a wide measure of discretion. Other than these few provisions, the Constitution that emerged from the Philadelphia Convention gave no attention to civil liberties.

When Colonel Mason suggested to the Convention that a committee be formed to draft "a Bill of Rights"—a task that could be accomplished "in a few hours"—the representatives of the various states offered little discussion on the motion and voted almost unanimously against it. The Bill of Rights, of course, was ratified only after the first Congress and president had been elected.

For the founders, liberty meant something different from democracy; it meant liberty to invest and trade and carry out the matters of business and enjoy the security of property without encroachment by king or populace. The civil liberties designed to give all individuals the right to engage actively in public affairs were of no central concern to the delegates and, as noted, were summarily voted down.

When asking how democratic the Constitution is, we need look not only at the Constitution but also at what we mean by "democracy," for different definitions have been ascribed to the term. Let us say that democracy is a system of governance that represents, both in form *and content*, the desires and interests of the ruled. This definition is more meaningful for the twentieth century—and at the same time somewhat closer to the eighteenth-century one—than the currently propagated view that reduces democracy to a set of procedures and "rules of the game." Democracy is a *social order* with a social class content—which is why the framers so disliked it. What they feared about democracy was not its forms but its content, the idea that the decisions of government might be of substantive benefit to the popular class at the expense of their own.

In a democracy, the people exercise a measure of control by electing their representatives and by subjecting them to the check of periodic elections, open criticism, and removal from office. In addition, a democratic people should be able to live without fear of want, enjoying freedom from economic, as well as political, oppression. In a real democracy, the material conditions of people's lives should be humane and roughly equal. It was this democratic vision that loomed as a nightmare for the Founding Fathers and for so many of their spiritual descendants today.

Some people argue that democracy is simply a system of rules for playing the game, which allows some measure of mass participation and government accountability, and that the Constitution is a kind of rule book. One should not try to impose, as a precondition of democracy, particular class relations, economic philosophies, or other substantive arrangements on this open-ended game. This argument certainly does reduce democracy to a game. It presumes that formal rules can exist in a meaningful way independently of substantive realities. Whether procedural rights are violated or enjoyed, whether one is treated by law as pariah or prince, depends largely on material realities that extend beyond a written constitution or other formal guarantees of law. Whether a political system is democratic depends not only on its procedures but on its substantive outputs, that is, the actual material benefits and costs of policy and the kind of social justice, or injustice, that is propagated. By this view, a government that pursues policies that by design or neglect are so inequitable as to deny people the very conditions of life, is not democratic, no matter how many competitive elections it holds.

The twentieth-century concept of social justice, involving something more than procedural liberties, is afforded no place in the eighteenth-century Constitution. The Constitution says nothing about those conditions of life that have come to be treated by many people as essential human rights—for instance, freedom from hunger; the right to decent housing, medical care, and education regardless of ability to pay; the right to gainful employment, safe working conditions, and a clean, nontoxic environment. Under the Constitution, equality is treated as a *procedural* right without a *substantive* content. Thus, "equality of opportunity" means equality of opportunity to move ahead competitively and become unequal to others; it means a chance to get in the game and best others rather than to enjoy an equal distribution and use of the resources needed for the maintenance of community life.

If the founders sought to "check power with power," they seemed chiefly concerned with restraining mass power, while assuring the perpetuation of their own class power. They supposedly had a "realistic" opinion of the self-interested and rapacious nature of human beings—readily evidenced when they talked about the common people—yet they held a remarkably sanguine view of the self-interested impulses of their own class, which they saw as being inhabited by industrious, trustworthy, and virtuous men. Recall Hamilton's facile reassurance that the rich will "check the unsteadiness" of the poor and will themselves "ever maintain good government" by being given a "distinct permanent share" in it. Power corrupts others but somehow has the opposite effect on the rich and the wellborn.

If the Constitution is so blatantly elitist, how did it manage to win enough popular support for ratification? First, it should be noted that it did not have a wide measure of support, initially being opposed in most of the states.* But the same superiority of wealth, leadership, organization, control of the press, and control of political office that allowed the rich to monopolize the Philadelphia Convention worked with similar effect in the ratification campaign. Superior wealth also enabled the Federalists to bribe, intimidate, and, in other ways, pressure and discourage opponents of the Constitution. At the same time, there were some elements in the laboring class, especially those who hoped to profit from employment in shipping and export trades, who supported ratification.[26]

Above all, it should be pointed out that the Constitution never was submitted to popular ratification. There was no national referendum and none in the states. Ratification was by state convention composed of elected delegates, the majority of whom were drawn from the more affluent strata. The voters who took part in the selection of delegates were subjected to a variety of property restrictions. In addition, the poor, even if enfranchised, carried all the liabilities that have caused them to be underrepresented in elections before and since: a lack of information and organization, illiteracy, a sense of being unable to have any effect on events, and a feeling that none of the candidates represented their interests. There were also the problems of relatively inaccessible polls and the absence of a secret ballot. Even if two-thirds or more of the adult white males could vote for delegates, as might have been the case in most states, probably not more than 20 percent actually did.[27]

In sum, the framers laid the foundation for a national government, but it was one that fit the specifications of the propertied class. They wanted protection from popular uprisings, from fiscal uncertainty and

[26] See Jackson Turner Main, *The Antifederalists* (Chapel Hill: University of North Carolina Press, 1961). Beard also mentions the northern workers who supported the move for stronger manufacturing and shipping protections; Beard, *An Economic Interpretation*, pp. 44-45. Apparently for some latter-day apologists, suggestions that *workers* supported the Constitution from direct economic interest is an acceptable datum, but that merchants, manufacturers, landowners, speculators, and creditors did so is a contention bred of the crudest economic determinism.

[27] See the studies cited by Beard, *An Economic Interpretation*, p. 242 ff.

* For another view of the ratification process and the question of popular support for the Constitution, see Alfred F. Young's essay in this volume—EDS.

irregularities in trade and currency, from trade barriers between states, from economic competition by more powerful foreign governments, and from attacks by the poor on property and on creditors. The Constitution was consciously designed as a conservative document, elaborately equipped with a system of minority checks and vetoes, making it hard to enact sweeping popular reforms or profound structural changes, and easy for entrenched interests to endure. It provided ample power to build the services and protections of state needed by a growing capitalist class but not the power for a transition of rule to a different class or to the public as a whole.

With some democratizing changes, including the direct election of the Senate and the enfranchisement of women, the Constitution fashioned in 1787 has served its intended purpose. During the industrial strife of the late nineteenth century, when the state militias proved unreliable and state legislatures too responsive to the demands of workers, the military power of the federal government was used repeatedly to suppress labor insurgency. Where would the robber barons have been without a Constitution that provided them with the forceful services of the U.S. Army? [28]

Similarly, for over seventy years, the Supreme Court wielded a minority veto on social welfare, unionization, and taxation, preventing reform legislation that had been enacted in European countries decades earlier. The Court became—and with momentary exceptions remains—what the founders intended it to be, a nonelective branch staffed by persons of elitist political, legal, and business backgrounds, exercising a preponderantly conservative influence as guardian of existing class and property relations.

The Senate today qualifies as the "tinsel aristocracy" that Jefferson scorned, composed mostly of persons with large financial holdings, many of them millionaires, who vote their own interests with shameless regularity. The House is subdivided into a network of special-interest subcommittees, dominated by the concerns of banking, agribusiness, and big corporations, in what has become almost a parody of Madison's lesson on how to divide power in order to fragment mass pressures and protect the propertied few.[29]

The system of popular elections, an institution most of the founders never liked, has been safely captured by two political parties that are financed by moneyed interests and dedicated to the existing

---

[28] See William Preston, Jr., *Aliens and Dissenters* (Cambridge, Mass.: Harvard University Press, 1963); Jeremy Brecher, *Strike!* (Greenwich, Conn.: Fawcett, 1974).

[29] For a fuller exposition of these points see my *Democracy for the Few*, 3rd ed. (New York: St. Martin's Press, 1980).

corporate social order. In modern times, especially at the national level, men of property have demonstrated their adeptness at financing elections, running for office, getting elected, and influencing those who are elected, in ways that would warm the heart of the most conservative Federalist. Electoral politics is largely a rich man's game and the property qualifications—as translated into campaign costs—are far steeper today than in 1787.[30]

The endeavor the framers began in Philadelphia, for a stronger central government to serve the commercial and industrial class, has continued and accelerated. As industrial capitalism has expanded at home and abroad, the burden of subsidizing its endeavors and providing the military force needed to protect its markets, resources, and client states has fallen disproportionately on that level of government which is national and international in scope—the federal—and on that branch which is best suited to carry out the necessary technical, organizational, and military tasks—the executive. The important decisions increasingly are being made in federal departments and corporate boardrooms and in the advisory committees that are linked to the upper echelons of the executive branch, staffed by public policy makers and private representatives of the major industries. I described this in an earlier work:

> One might better think of ours as a dual political system. First, there is the *symbolic* political system centering around electoral and representative activities including party conflicts, voter turnout, political personalities, public pronouncements, official role-playing and certain ambiguous presentations of some of the public issues which bestir Presidents, governors, mayors and their respective legislatures. Then there is the *substantive* political system, involving multibillion-dollar contracts, tax write-offs, protections, rebates, grants, loss compensations, subsidies, leases, giveaways and the whole vast process of budgeting, legislating, advising, regulating, protecting and servicing major producer interests, now bending or ignoring the law on behalf of the powerful, now applying it with full punitive vigor against heretics and "troublemakers." The symbolic system is highly visible, taught in the schools, dissected by academicians, gossiped about by newsmen. The substantive system is seldom heard of or accounted for.[31]

[30] Ibid.
[31] Ibid., p. 304.

By offering well-protected havens for powerful special interests, by ignoring substantive rights and outcomes, by mobilizing the wealth and force of the state in a centralizing and property-serving way, by making democratic change difficult, the Constitution has served well an undemocratic military-industrial corporate structure. The rule of the "minority faction," the "persons of substance," the "propertied interest," the "rich and the well-born"—to mention a few of the ways the founders described their class—has prevailed. The delegates would have every reason to be satisfied with the enduring nature of their work.

4

Does the Constitution "Secure These Rights"?

Walter Berns

The Constitution is more democratic today than in the past and promising (or threatening) to become still more democratic. Senators are no longer even formally selected by state legislatures but are popularly elected. Presidents continue formally to be chosen by a few presidential electors, but these electors themselves are chosen by the voters; except for an occasional maverick eager to call attention to himself at no cost to anyone else, they have long since given up their nominal independence. The various restrictions placed on the suffrage by state constitutions, statutes, parties, and practices, have been removed over the course of time by formal amendment of the Constitution as well as by federal statute and Supreme Court decision. States are supposed to apportion both houses of their legislatures according to the democratic principle that allows "a majority of the people of a state [to] elect a majority of that state's legislators."[1] Not only are elections more popular, but the people now play—or are entitled to play—a greater role in the selection of the candidates to run in those elections: the party convention has been superseded by the party primary, the bosses by the people, the smoke-filled big-city hotel room by the open pellucid spaces of rural New Hampshire. If, then, democracy means government by the people, we have more of it today—formally at least—than in the past.

Not only does the Constitution now require, as well as permit, more democracy in the political process, but it has been interpreted to require a greater degree of democracy—understood here as equality—in American society. The equal protection of the laws has come increasingly to mean laws that draw no distinctions: between black

[1] Reynolds v. Sims, 377 U.S. 533, 565 (1964).

and white, male and female, citizen and alien, resident and non-resident, wed and unwed, or legitimate and illegitimate.[2]

The Constitution is not, however, sufficiently democratic to satisfy everyone. Birch Bayh and a majority (but not a two-thirds majority) of his Senate colleagues look upon the electoral college as an anachronism, a vestige of a less democratic past that must be swept away in favor of direct, popular election. What concerns them is not so much the remote possibility that a president will be elected without a majority of popular votes, or even that the electoral college will be unable to produce a winner (thus throwing an election into the House of Representatives), but rather what they understand to be the principle underlying this method of choosing presidents. That principle, they say, is undemocratic. In these democratic times, they insist, only a popular majority can bestow legitimacy; indeed, as was made clear in the 1979 hearings on his bill to abolish the electoral college, Bayh himself would prefer a system designed to produce a popularly elected president to one designed to produce a better qualified president.[3]

James Abourezk, formerly a senator from South Dakota, would go further in this direction; he would amend the Constitution to permit not direct election but direct legislation. In his scheme, 3 percent of the voters would be empowered to initiate legislation by putting a proposal on the ballot which, without amendment, would become law if it gained the support of a popular majority in the next general election. Like Bayh, Abourezk and the cosponsors of this proposed constitutional amendment, Senators Mark Hatfield and Mike Gravel, are concerned with the form rather than the end of government. One might say that they are concerned primarily with process —it must be as directly democratic as possible—and only secondarily, if at all, with what comes out of that process. They stand for direct popular rule, which in practice, presumably, would mean simple majoritarianism mitigated or limited only by the power of judicial review.

During the Warren years especially, the Supreme Court was moved by a similar spirit and, as a result, managed to produce not

---

[2] See, in addition to the host of racial classification cases, Frontiero v. Richardson, 411 U.S. 677 (1973); Sugarman v. Dougall, 413 U.S. 634 (1973); Shapiro v. Thompson, 394 U.S. 618 (1969); Eisenstadt v. Baird, 405 U.S. 438 (1972); and Trimble v. Gordon, 430 U.S. 762 (1977).

[3] U.S. Congress, Senate, Subcommittee on the Constitution of the Committee on the Judiciary, Hearings on S.J. Res. 28, *Direct Popular Election of the President and Vice President of the United States*, 96th Congress, 1st session, March 27, 30, April 3, 9, 1979, p. 137.

only a more democratic, that is, majoritarian, Constitution, but a somewhat fanciful account of history. "The conception of political equality," said Justice William O. Douglas, "from the Declaration of Independence to Lincoln's Gettysburg Address, to the Fifteenth, Seventeenth, and Nineteenth Amendments can mean only one thing—one person, one vote."[4] This version of this one aspect of history became the official one when, the following year, Chief Justice Warren quoted and reiterated it in his opinion for the Court in the second-chamber apportionment cases.[5]

How democratic is the Constitution? It is not yet democratic enough for these men. It is not yet democratic enough for those who insist that democracy requires an equal distribution of material goods. It is not yet democratic enough for anyone who, contrary to original practice, insists that this is the first and most important question to ask about a political system.

We call ourselves a constitutional or liberal democracy, and occasionally, if we are careless or hurried, simply a democracy. The most famous book about us is entitled *Democracy in America*, but, unlike many contemporary writers and politicians, Alexis de Tocqueville, the author of that book, understood democracy to be one of several "régimes" (to adopt his term) under which liberty, or the rights of man, might—or, depending on circumstance and condition, might *not*—be secured. He was continually mindful of the purpose or end of government and analyzed the strengths and weaknesses of democracy and constitution in that light. In this respect, he resembled the men of our founding generation, not only James Madison, James Wilson, and Alexander Hamilton, but, what is frequently overlooked and sometimes denied, Patrick Henry, Luther Martin, and Melancton Smith as well. All of them, Federalists and Antifederalists alike, took their bearings from the Declaration of Independence with its statement of self-evident truth that government is instituted in order to secure the rights with which all men are equally endowed. None of them made the easy, and, according to the Declaration, the improper, assumption that democracy was the only form of government under which these rights could be secured. (This is discussed in more detail later.) How democratic is the Constitution? That is not the central question; at best it is a subordinate question.

---

[4] Gray v. Sanders, 372 U.S. 368, 381 (1963).
[5] Reynolds v. Sims, 377 U.S. 533, 558 (1964).

The Issues at Ratification

Nothing I have said about the Federalists and Antifederalists is intended to minimize their differences. With respect to the point at issue in their debates—whether the Constitution should be ratified—these differences were decisive and were understood to be decisive.

The Antifederalists' objections to the Constitution are too well known to require elaboration here. Specifically, they objected to what they saw as a consolidating of the states with the consequent undermining of their authority; the absence of a bill of rights; an inadequate system of representation (too few members of the House, they insisted); the failure adequately to separate powers; and, to cite one other objection, too powerful an executive. Generally, they complained that the Constitution would take power from the people and put it in the hands of a favored few.

There is, thus, some reason to see the ratification struggle as a contest between democrats and aristocrats. Did not the arch-Federalist Hamilton openly call for a chief executive who would serve during good behavior, with a monarch's absolute veto on all laws; should this not cause one to suspect his professions of attachment to republicanism? Did he not find even the Virginia plan, which provided the basis for the Constitution, too democratic, referring to it as "pork still, with a little change of sauce"? He did indeed, and similar if less pungent statements were uttered by other Federalists. For eulogia on the "genius of democracy," one has to turn to the speeches of Patrick Henry, for one, and he opposed the Constitution: it has an "awful squinting," he said; "it squints toward monarchy." Removed from their contexts, however, these statements serve principally to conceal the issue being debated by Hamilton, Henry, and their respective associates.

They were not debating the source of legitimate government; that, both parties agreed, was in the people. When men are by nature equal, no one may rule another without his consent; there can be no American coin with the inscription *Dei gratia Regina* or *Dei gratia Rex*. Interestingly, it is to the agreement on this fundamental point that we owe the public character of the ratification debates in the several states; the Federalists and Antifederalists were contending for a consent that only the people could give. It was otherwise in Canada during that country's confederation debates in the 1860s. Precisely because it was understood that the Canadian decision was one to be made in principle by the queen, who was queen by the grace of God, and in practice by her ministers, the debates took place in the various provincial parliaments, not "out of doors."

Nor, as already mentioned, were the Federalists and Antifederalists debating the proper end of government, one side contending for a Christian commonwealth and the other for a liberal state, or, to state this in terms of the Declaration, one side insisting that government be empowered to define the happiness that the governed were enjoined to seek, and the other insisting that each man had a natural right to define for himself the happiness he was entitled to pursue. By 1787, the "throne-and-altar" Americans either had gone to Canada, where even today some descendants can be found marching under the banner of United Empire Loyalists, or were content to remain silent.

What the Federalists and Antifederalists were debating was the form of government best calculated to secure the rights of all Americans. The Federalists especially were impressed by the difficulties of this. The simple republican form could not be relied on to produce free government. Indeed, it was impossible "to read the history of the petty republics of Greece and Italy without feeling sensations of horror and disgust at the distractions with which they were continually agitated, and at the rapid succession of revolutions by which they were kept in a state of perpetual vibration between the extremes of tyranny and anarchy."[6] The Antifederalists tended, on the whole, to be content with the Articles of Confederation, under which the real power of government was exercised at the state level. They conceded the need for minor amendments, as well as the need for union, but only as a defense against foreign nations and as mediator between states. To the Federalists, however, the states resembled too closely those petty Greek and Italian republics and were doomed to suffer the same fate. To rely on the traditional republican forms, they argued, would only strengthen the case of those who insisted that republican government and civil liberty were incompatible.[7] What they proposed in their place were the newly devised models of a "more perfect [republican] structure."

> The science of politics . . . like most other sciences, has received great improvements. The efficacy of various principles is now well understood, which were either not known at all, or imperfectly known to the ancients. The regular distribution of power into distinct departments; the introduction of legislative balances and checks; the institution of courts composed of judges holding their offices during

---

[6] Alexander Hamilton, James Madison, and John Jay, *The Federalist Papers*, ed. Clinton Rossiter (New York: New American Library, 1961), No. 9.
[7] Ibid.

good behavior; the representation of the people in the legislature by deputies of their own election: these are wholly
new discoveries, or have made their principal progress
towards perfection in modern times. . . . To this catalogue
of circumstances that tend to the amelioration of popular
systems of civil government, I shall venture, however novel
it may appear to some, to add one more . . . I mean the
ENLARGEMENT of the ORBIT within which such systems
are to revolve. . . .[8]

These various institutional arrangements were intended to provide
a "republican remedy for the diseases most incident to republican
government." If men were angels, "Publius" says in *Federalist*
No. 51, no government would be necessary; if one could trust the
governors to be angelic, there would be no need to institute either
external or internal controls. In this abode of men, there would have
to be government, and experience proved that the government would
have to be controlled. "A dependence on the people is, no doubt,
the primary control on the government; but experience has taught
mankind the necessity of auxiliary precautions." The precautions
they took, and for which they were indebted to the new political
science, were intended to do what the people could not be expected
to do, namely, provide restraints on popular majorities.

The novelty attributed by Publius to the federal judiciary can
only be understood in this context. It was the judges' duty to be
"faithful guardians of the Constitution," and the Federalists expected
the most dangerous invasions of it to be "instigated by the major
voice of the community."[9] In Britain—at least in the Britain that figures in Montesquieu's description of separated or balanced powers—
the power of the people would be balanced by that of the nobles, and,
failing that, it could be offset by the monarch. In America there were
neither nobles nor kings. Hence, as I have argued elsewhere, in the
American system of separated powers, the independent judiciary,
exercising the new power of judicial review, was intended to take
the place of the hereditary monarch, with his absolute veto, and the
aristocratic House of Lords.

What Montesquieu sought to accomplish by dividing the
legislative power between two factions—the people and the
nobility—the American Constitution seeks to accomplish by
means of a written document that limits the legislative
power by specifying "exceptions to the legislative authority;

---

[8] Ibid.
[9] *Federalist* No. 78.

such for instance, as that it shall pass no bills of attainder, no ex post facto laws, and the like." By enforcing these limitations, the Supreme Court will, in its way, maintain a balance between the factions that will arise in America, not between nobles and the people, but between few and many or creditors and debtors. What we have in America is a constitutional balance in the form of a limited Constitution, and the Court is very much a part of that balance.[10]

Publius may prefer to describe judicial review as a "republican" institution, but only in an impoverished political lexicon, one that offers no respectable alternative, could it be described as democratic so long as it functions as it was intended. Had Publius been more candid, he would have said that in judicial review we behold a *republican* remedy for the diseases more incident to *democratic* government.

The Concept of Representation

This amended formulation surely comes closer to expressing the Federalists' idea of representation and the disease it was intended to cure. Both they and the Antifederalists spoke in favor of representation but understood by it exactly opposite things. Indeed, it is no exaggeration to say that the ratification debate was essentially a debate about representation.

In *Federalist* No. 9, as pointed out earlier, Publius makes the claim that an improved science of politics has made it possible for the first time to appreciate the "efficacy of various principles [that] were either not known at all, or imperfectly known to the ancients." Among these, he lists "the representation of the people in the legislature by deputies of their own election." That, to say the least, is a puzzling statement. What was new about representation? In what respect was American representation new? For the Federalists, representation was a way of keeping the people out of government. It was this concept that the earlier friends of republican government did not understand. As Publius concedes in a later number of *The Federalist*, they were familiar with the principle but did not know how to apply it:

> It is clear that the principle of representation was neither unknown to the ancients nor wholly overlooked in their political constitutions. The true distinction between these

---

[10] Walter Berns, "The Least Dangerous Branch But Only If . . .," in Leonard J. Theberge, ed., *The Judiciary in a Democratic Society* (Lexington, Massachusetts, and Toronto: Lexington Books, 1979), p. 8. The statement quoted is from *Federalist* No. 78.

and the American government lies *in the total exclusion of
the people in their collective capacity,* from any share in the
latter, and not in the *total exclusion of the representatives
of the people* from the administration of the *former.* [Emphasis in the original.] [11]

The American system, he says, is vastly superior, but "to insure to
this advantage its full effect, we must be careful not to separate it
from the other advantage, of an extensive territory." An extensive
territory makes it possible to keep the people, in their collective
capacity, out of the government, or out of any direct participation
in government. They elect representatives but the persons they elect
do not represent them!

What this means can be understood by contrasting it with the
Antifederalists' view. Here is Melancton Smith speaking against the
Constitution in the New York ratifying convention:

> The idea that naturally suggests itself to our minds, when
> we speak of representatives, is, that they resemble those
> they represent. They should be a true picture of the
> people. . . . [12]

Another term frequently employed by the Antifederalists was
"mirror"; a representative body should be a "mirror" or a "reflection"
of the people. To employ an etymological device, a representative
body should present the people again, that is to say, it should
re-present them. It was because the Antifederalists wanted representation in this sense that they objected to a consolidation of the
states under a government that would exercise power over a huge
territory and would comprehend too large and too diverse a population; this explains as well their calls for rotation in office, annual
elections, and a larger number of representatives. Ideally, there
should be *no* representatives. The people should themselves assemble
and give themselves laws; they should *present* themselves in the
legislative assembly. Failing that (and the Antifederalists had to
concede that even the states were too large for direct democracy),
there should be *many* representatives, for only a large body could
provide an accurate reflection of the people.

To the same end, the Antifederalists called for responsible representation and meant by it a representation "responsive" to the will
of the people and immediately answerable to the people. Here is
"Centinel" writing in *The Independent Gazetteer* of Philadelphia:

---

[11] *Federalist* No. 63.

[12] Jonathan Elliot, *The Debates in the Several State Conventions on the Adoption
of the Federal Constitution* (Philadelphia: Lippincott, 1888), vol. 2, p. 245.

The highest responsibility is to be attained in a simple structure of government. . . . If you complicate the plan by various orders, the people will be perplexed and divided in their sentiments about the source of abuses or misconduct. . . . But if, imitating the constitution of Pennsylvania, you vest all the legislative power in one body of men (separating the executive and judicial) elected for a short period, and necessarily excluded by rotation from permanency . . . you will create the most perfect responsibility; for then, whenever the people feel a grievance, they cannot mistake the authors, and will apply the remedy with certainty and effect, discarding them at the next election. This tie of responsibility will obviate all the dangers apprehended from a single legislature, and will the best secure the rights of the people.[13]

Responsibility Demanded by Democracy

This same theme is sounded throughout Antifederalist literature. In the proposed Constitution, Patrick Henry said, "there is no true responsibility"; what is required in a democracy is "real not imaginary responsibility."[14] The same sort of objections were made in New York; no responsibility can be expected from a body elected for two years, "Cato" complained, or from so small a number of representatives. The Constitution's first article departs from "safe democratic principles," and this is especially true of its provisions for the Senate. The mode in which senators will be appointed as well as their long duration in office "will lead to the establishment of an aristocracy."[15]

While they might have protested the use of the term "aristocracy" to describe their idea of representation, the Federalists made no secret of the fact that they wanted uncommon men to be elected; they were sometimes willing to have them referred to as a "natural aristocracy." In a large republic with relatively few representatives, they could expect the people—even a democratic people—to choose men distinguished by their virtue and talents. They saw this as altogether necessary and proper. The persons elected to public office should not reflect the people who choose them; on the contrary, they should be a "chosen body of citizens, whose wisdom may best discern

---

[13] Cecilia Kenyon, ed., *The Antifederalists* (Indianapolis: Bobbs-Merrill, 1966), pp. 7-8.

[14] Elliot, *Debates*, vol. 3, p. 61.

[15] Paul L. Ford, *Essays on the Constitution of the United States* (New York: Burt Franklin, 1970, reprint of the 1892 edition), p. 267.

the true interest of their country and whose patriotism and love of justice will be least likely to sacrifice it to temporary or partial considerations."[16]

In deference to the Antifederalists, Publius admits the need for responsible representatives, but, somewhat playfully one suspects, he asserts that there can be no responsibility under a system of frequent elections. This remark, he says, will appear to be not only new but "paradoxical";[17] indeed it does, since it is the exact opposite of the commonly held opinion. His explanation follows immediately: the people cannot hold their representatives responsible for decisions or policies as to which they, the people, are incapable of making sound judgments, and some, but not all, of the business of government will be of this order of complexity. With respect to policy, Publius argues, there will be a distinction between the public's opinion of what ought to be done, on the one hand, and what is truly in the interest of the country. Representatives ought to be responsible to the latter, or, to use the term employed by Publius, they ought to be responsible to the "collective and permanent welfare" of the country. Responsibility in this sense depends in part on their being somewhat independent of their constituents; there is very little independence under a system of annual elections.

My argument is that the ratification debate was essentially a debate about representation, a subject made up of many elements, with many ramifications. This was understood well by both parties and understood perfectly by their leading members: They knew what was at stake. On no other subject were they so sharply divided. The respective parties favored a complex government and a simple government, a large republic and many small ones, few legislators and many, infrequent and indirect elections as opposed to frequent and direct. The Antifederalists accused the Federalists of favoring aristocracy and the Federalists implicitly admitted it. What the Federalists described as disease, the Antifederalists accepted as a sign of health. Yet, both sides wanted liberty and security for the rights of man.

The Weight of Political Authority

The Antifederalists were no more simple majoritarian democrats than the Federalists were aristocrats in any traditional sense; it is a serious mistake to see the issue at stake in 1787–1788 in these terms. There

---

[16] *Federalist* No. 10.

[17] *Federalist* No. 63.

was no American nobility, and there was no possibility of establishing anything equivalent to a House of Lords; both parties understood this. John Adams contrived a system of separated powers in which the balance between the two legislative branches would, he hoped, reflect a balance of social orders; but Adams was not at Philadelphia when the Constitution was being written and his system was rejected. Madison, in the course of defending the small number of senators, argued that that body would be given "weight" by its small size and by the powers given it, not by the families represented in it. It was John Dickinson of Delaware who "adhered to the opinion that the Senate ought to be composed of a large number, and that their influence (from family weight and other causes) would be increased thereby."

Madison disagreed. He put it this way:

> The more the representatives of the people [are] multiplied, the more they [partake] of the infirmities of their constituents, the more liable they [become] to be divided among themselves either from their own indiscretions or the artifices of the opposite factions, and of course the less capable of fulfilling their trust. *When the weight of a set of men depends merely on their personal characters; the greater the number the greater the weight. When it depends on the degree of political authority lodged in them the smaller the number the greater the weight.*[18]

James Wilson, in support of Madison, pointed out that the British system "cannot be our model"; America lacked the "material" for it. There were no noble families, no "laws of entails and of primogeniture," and American manners, laws, and the "whole genius of the people" are opposed to them.[19]

The Antifederalists agreed. In regard to Britain, "Centinel" said, "they have a powerful hereditary nobility, and real distinctions of rank," but such are lacking in America.[20] "We have not materials for such a government in this country," said William Grayson in the Virginia debates.[21] Lacking such social "materials"—that is to say, in the absence of anything resembling a noble class to balance legislatively against the people and thereby achieve the moderation that Montesquieu saw in the British system—the principal Federalists, led

---

[18] Max Farrand, ed., *The Records of the Federal Convention of 1787* (New Haven: Yale University Press, 1937), vol. 1, p. 152. (Italics not in the original.)

[19] Ibid., pp. 151, 153, 154.

[20] Kenyon, *Antifederalists*, p. 6.

[21] Elliot, *Debates*, vol. 3, p. 279.

by Madison, sought to substitute what Herbert Storing called "constitutional weight." By this he meant that the "weight" of the Senate will depend less on the qualities the senators bring with them, so to speak, and more on the powers they are given when they take their seats.[22] By means of constitutional institutions, the Federalists hoped to produce and to find a place for a "natural aristocracy." They were not, to coin a term, doctrinaire aristocrats, if such a breed exists.

Nor were the Antifederalists simple majoritarians. Their advocacy of a simple, or a simpler, democracy cannot be severed from their advocacy of small and simple republics; in other words, their views on representation and size of country—and, as we shall see, *character* of country—were inseparable. This has implications that, when understood, might cause their champions among twentieth-century academics to see them in a different light. The Antifederalists were opposed to the Constitution, but, contrary to their reputation in some quarters, they were not simply or essentially "men of little faith"; they were *for* something. They advocated the kind of democracy that few, if any, contemporary friends of democracy do. This becomes clear in their discussions of what they opposed.

They opposed a standing army. "Who can deny," asked "Philadelphiensis," but that the *"president general* will be a *king* to all intents and purposes, and one of the most dangerous kind too; a king elected to command a standing army?"[23] This objection was repeatedly voiced during the course of the ratification debates, and nowhere better than in the words of Richard Henry Lee of Virginia. The great object of a free people, Lee wrote under the name "The Federal Farmer," was to form and administer their government so as to create confidence in it, especially among the "sensible and virtuous part of the community."

This confidence carries with it a freely given consent to the laws; the alternative to freely given consent is an "expensive military force."[24] The general rule is, he wrote in another place and under his own name, that government must exist "if not by persuasion, then by force." He and his colleagues argued that not in

---

[22] I have profited enormously from an association with Storing that began in 1950 when we were graduate students together at the University of Chicago and ended only with his death in 1977. Not only did I learn from our many conversations on the subject of the American founding, but in preparing this paper I enjoyed the benefit of possessing the final draft of his long introduction to his soon-to-be published edition of the Antifederalist papers.

[23] Kenyon, *Antifederalists,* p. 72.

[24] *Letters of a Federal Farmer* (Richard Henry Lee), no. 3, in Paul L. Ford, ed., *Pamphlets on the Constitution of the United States* (New York: Da Capo Press, 1968, a republication of the 1888 edition), p. 294.

the United States as a whole but only within each individual state was a freely given consent possible. Only in each state will the people possess knowledge of the men they elect to office. "But remove this opinion, which must fall with a knowledge of characters in so widely extended a country, and force then becomes necessary to secure the purposes of civil government. . . ."[25] The same point was made in Massachusetts by "Agrippa," who insisted that history and experience prove that free government is not possible in an extensive territory including diverse peoples. "Hence arises in most nations of extensive territories the necessity of armies, to cure the defect of the laws."[26]

Unacceptable Conditions of Government

Smallness, however, was understood by them to be merely a necessary and not a sufficient condition of free republican government; it is the additional conditions that would not be acceptable today—and proved to be unacceptable in 1788. One of these is a homogeneous population. Agrippa, for example, in the context of arguing that the national government cannot be trusted with the power to naturalize aliens, contrasted the happiness of the "eastern" states with the situation in Pennsylvania, which had permitted open immigration.

> Pennsylvania has chosen to receive all that would come there. Let any indifferent person judge whether that state in point of morals, education, energy is equal to any of the eastern states [which, "by keeping separate from the foreign mixtures" have] acquired their present greatness in the course of a century and a half, and have preserved their religion and morals.[27]

Pennsylvania may be willing to receive foreigners, "yet reasons of equal weight may induce other states, differently circumstanced, to keep their blood pure."

There must be a similarity not only of national origin but of manners and sentiments; this is possible only if, in addition, there is a similarity of interests. Thus, in speech after speech, in state after state, we see praise of the "sturdy yeomanry," or of people of the middling sort, or a homogeneity of simplicity. In short, the Antifederalists were inclined to echo Jefferson's praise of a simple agri-

---

[25] Richard Henry Lee, "Letter to————," April 28, 1788, in James Curtis Ballagh, *The Letters of Richard Henry Lee* (New York: Macmillan, 1914), vol. 2, p. 464.

[26] Agrippa (John Winthrop?), no. 12, in Ford, *Essays*, p. 92.

[27] Agrippa, no. 9, in Ford, *Essays*, p. 79.

cultural society.[28] The life devoted to commerce, and especially foreign commerce, is one that leads to extremes of wealth, a taste for luxury, and a dissolute people. "It was asked in the Reign of Charles the 2d of England," that sturdy patriot Samuel Adams pointed out, "how shall we turn the Minds of the People from an Attention to their Liberties. The Answer was, by making them extravagant, luxurious, effeminate." Adams wanted, and once thought it possible to build in Boston, "the *Christian* Sparta."[29] In a word, republican government rests on civic virtue which can be promoted and perpetuated only in the small republic and only under a government empowered to pay attention to such matters. I mean by this that the Antifederalists were the ones inclined to deplore the Constitution's prohibition of religious tests for officeholders[30] and beyond that to call, not for civil religion in an older sense, but for the public promotion of good morals and manners; this depended on public support for religious institutions. There would continue to be a good deal of "preaching" in these small republics.[31]

The Antifederalists were *for* democracy; they were *for* direct representation of the people and majority rule; but they were also for a homogeneous society in which majority would scarcely differ from minority. Publius had this in mind when, in the famous tenth

---

[28] Jefferson, *Notes on the State of Virginia*, Query 19 (New York: Harper Torchbooks, 1964), p. 157. Melancton Smith, in the New York ratifying convention, in the course of stating his objections to the system of representation under the proposed Constitution, complained that a "substantial yeoman . . . will hardly ever be chosen." He then went on as follows: "I do not mean to declaim against the great, and charge them indiscriminately with want of principle and honesty. The same passions and prejudices govern all men. The circumstances in which men are placed in a great measure give a cast to the human character. Those in middling circumstances have less temptation; they are inclined by habit, and the company with whom they associate, to set bounds to their passions and appetites. If this is not sufficient, the want of means to gratify them will be a restraint: they are obliged to employ their time in their respective callings; hence the substantial yeomanry of the country are more temperate, of better morals, and less ambition, than the great." Elliot, *Debates*, vol. 2, p. 247.

[29] Samuel Adams, "Letter to John Scollay," December 30, 1780, in Cushing, ed., *The Writings of Samuel Adams* (1908), vol. 4, pp. 237-238.

[30] Amos Singletary of Massachusetts complained that there was no provision that men in power should have any religion; "and though he hoped to see Christians, yet by the Constitution, a Papist, or an Infidel, was as eligible as they." Elliot, *Debates*, vol. 2, p. 44.

[31] See, for example, Agrippa, in Ford, *Essays*, pp. 65, 79, 92. An insistence that the states be permitted to continue to foster religion in one way or another surfaced in the debates on the First Amendment in the first Congress. See Walter Berns, *The First Amendment and the Future of American Democracy* (New York: Basic Books, 1976), chap. 1, and Gordon Wood, *The Creation of the American Republic, 1776-1787* (Chapel Hill: University of North Carolina Press, 1969), chaps. 3 and 10.

Federalist essay, he said there are two methods of removing the causes of factions, one of them being to give "to every citizen the same opinions, the same passions, and the same interests." If this is not possible—and I think it is fair to say that the Antifederalists lost the debate because the majority of Americans in 1787–1788 realized that it was not possible by any desirable means—then another cure would have to be adopted. There would be factions; the public good depended on their being controlled, and, Publius said, "we well know that neither moral nor religious motives can be relied on as an adequate control." Hence he summed up: "From this view of the subject it may be concluded that a pure democracy, by which I mean a society consisting of a small number of citizens, who assemble and administer the government in person [or any close facsimile of this], can admit of no cure for the mischief of faction."[32]

Factions could, however, be controlled in a properly structured system, one that, among its other features, protects the equal right of everyone (however unequally endowed) to acquire property. In the large commercial republic, the animosity of factions will become the competition of interests. This competition will be peaceful because, all of them prospering to a greater or lesser extent—and the failure of the socialists to enlist the American working man is evidence of the extent to which this has occurred—the various factions will recognize a common interest in the preservation of a Constitution that secures everyone's right to prosper and, more importantly, live as free persons. The connection between economic and political liberty is one of the premises of the Constitution.

In voting to ratify the Constitution, Americans voted against the loose confederation of small, simple, virtuous, and democratic republics, and in favor of a strong, complex, and commercial republic, whose first object, Publius said, is "the protection of different and unequal faculties of acquiring property." Whether they knew it or not—and there can be no doubt that at least Publius knew it—they had voted to test the validity of the proposition advanced by the philosophers of natural rights—primarily John Locke and Montesquieu—that, when combined with certain institutional arrangements in the modern liberal state, commerce could serve as a substitute for morality.

Democracy as an Option

Since 1940, at least, when Merrill Jensen first published his popular study *The Articles of Confederation*, there has been a tendency among American historians to see the Constitution as the successful

---

[32] *Federalist* No. 10.

conclusion of a conservative or even counterrevolutionary backlash against the spirit and the works of the Revolution. (I am not unaware of the somewhat similar charges leveled earlier by Charles Beard or of the view, stemming from the Jacksonian period and the work of George Bancroft, that sees American history as a continual struggle between democracy and aristocracy.) That spirit found its theoretical expression in the Declaration of Independence and those works included, in addition to the successful war for independence, the Articles of Confederation.

The Articles, Jensen says, were the "natural outcome of the revolutionary movement [and the] constitutional expression of the philosophy of the Declaration of Independence."[33] This, Jensen implies rather than asserts, cannot be said of the Constitution of 1787; this Constitution is alleged to embody other principles and can be traced to another source. It was the work of "conservatives" who, albeit "in the name of the people," succeeded in supplanting the Articles with "a nationalistic government whose purpose in part was to thwart the will of the 'people' in whose name they acted."[34] The validity of these conclusions depends on his understanding of the Declaration of Independence, and, with all due respect, I must disagree with that understanding.

As indicated earlier, legitimacy rests on consent. Democracy is merely one of the forms to which an enlightened people can give their consent: institutions designed to translate the unguided will of the people directly into policy or law are not only *not* required by the Declaration but are only too likely to become "destructive" of the ends for which government is instituted. Because they understood this, neither the Federalists nor the Antifederalists believed in an unrestrained or unstructured majority rule. They sought security for the rights of man; democracy is not among those rights.

The people do have a right to choose democracy, but they also have a right to choose some other form of government. It is a self-evident truth that "whenever any form of government becomes destructive of these ends, it is the Right of the People to alter or to abolish it, and to institute new Government, laying its foundations on such principles and organizing its powers in such forms, as to them shall seem most likely to effect their Safety and Happiness." Contrary to Carl Becker,[35] I think that the Declaration does not con-

---

[33] Merrill Jensen, *The Articles of Confederation* (Madison: University of Wisconsin Press, 1940, 1976), p. 239.

[34] Ibid., p. 245.

[35] Carl Becker, *The Declaration of Independence* (New York: Vintage Books, 1942), p. 7.

tain a presumption against kings in general but only against tyrannical kings. A nontyrannical king—or prince, to use the Declaration's term—*may* be fit to rule a free people and may have the consent of the people.[36] They have a natural right to choose to be governed by him. It is when the choice of the form of government is being made that the majority rules; it is then that the will of the people must, as a matter of natural right, be ascertained.

> The majority, having, as has been shown, upon men's first entering into society, the whole power of the community naturally in them, may employ all that power in making laws for the community from time to time, and executing those laws by officers of their own appointing; and then the form of the government is a perfect democracy; or else may put the power of making laws into the hands of a few select men, and their heirs or successors: and then it is an oligarchy; or else into the hands of one man: and then it is a monarchy. . . .[37]

The Federalists—or, if you will, the "conservatives"—did not "thwart the will of the 'people' "; that will was expressed in 1787–1788. Having been persuaded by the Federalists, the people voted to adopt a form of government that, in their best judgment, would best secure their rights. By adopting that form of government, the majority put limits on themselves and future majorities, and they were entitled to do this.

A Defense of Majority Rule

Except on the basis of natural right, it is not easy, and may even be impossible, to provide a principled defense of majority rule, or, stated otherwise, to defend majority rule on the level of principle. Presumably such a defense would rest on an assertion of the equality of men; but in what respects are men equal—naturally equal—one to another? We all know that they are not equally intelligent, virtuous, godly, handsome, white, yellow, or black. Nor are they equally strong; unless the stronger can be taught that strength is not a legitimate claim to rule, they will rule. Not only will they rule, but the weak, in addition to being unable to resist in practice, will be unable to object in principle. The only respect in which all men are equal is in their possession of natural rights. It is from the fact of

---

[36] "A Prince, whose character is thus marked by every act which may define a Tyrant, is unfit to be a ruler of a free people."

[37] Locke, *The Second Treatise of Government*, sec. 132.

this equality of rights that the majority derives its right to determine the form of government under which all will live. The question put to the people on this founding occasion is, and can only be, under what form of government will rights best be secured?

In summary, majority rule can be justified only if men are equal; they are equal only in their possession of rights. A politics of equality must, therefore, be a politics concerned with rights; consequently, majority rule is legitimate rule only if in practice the majority respects the rights of the minority. Whatever might be the case with Bayh and Abourezk and any other advocates of simple majoritarianism, the American civil rights groups have always understood this, at least in America and for Americans; they owe it to themselves, as well as to the minorities involved, to remember that the principle applies elsewhere as well.

Two Ideas of Equality

How democratic is the Constitution? To ask that question suggests that a constitution should be judged primarily in terms of its responsiveness to public opinion. That, I have argued, is improper, contrary to the principles on the basis of which we declared our independence and assumed" among the powers of the earth, the separate and equal station to which the Laws of Nature and Nature's God" entitled us. To ask it as if it were the only question, or even the chief question, may deflect our attention from the rights for the security of which we formed a government. Indeed, the asking of it in that spirit may indicate that we have already forgotten the nature of those rights.

We once defined human rights in terms of freedom and the non-material (for even the property right was formulated as a right to acquire). There is a growing tendency to define these rights in terms of equality and the material. Thus, we hear it said that the essential human rights are "freedom from hunger, the right to decent housing, medical care and education regardless of ability to pay, the right to gainful employment, safe working conditions, a clean, nontoxic environment."[38] To secure human rights in the original sense required government to protect and respect the private realm; to secure the new human rights will require government to intervene in the private realm and eventually to destroy it. Those who now demand as a right the equal distribution of material goods will inevitably come to

---

[38] Michael Parenti, "The Constitution as an Elitist Document," in this volume.

demand (and in some cases have already demanded[39]) an equal right to the happiness these goods are supposed to bring, not a right to pursue happiness but the right to gain it. To secure this right will require government to declare war on human nature. The well-endowed (with intelligence, energy, beauty, or whatever) cannot be permitted to benefit, nor the unendowed to suffer, from nature's "injustice." Government can secure this new right to equality only by enlisting the assistance of the geneticists. Tocqueville foresaw this development:

> I think that democratic communities have a natural taste for freedom; left to themselves, they will seek it, cherish it, and view any privation of it with regret. But for equality their passion is ardent, insatiable, incessant, invincible; they call for equality in freedom; and if they cannot obtain that, they still call for equality in slavery.[40]

Our history has not been a struggle between democracy and aristocracy; it has been struggle between equality and liberty, or between the two ideas of equality.

The participants in this struggle know and have always known that, contrary to Gordon Wood, "there was and is [a] 'real' Constitution."[41] It was and is real in the sense that the struggle is carried on in its terms and categories, and sometimes over its terms and categories. (The Abolitionists in the nineteenth century knew this, and the advocates of the equal rights amendment know it today.) The Constitution is real in the sense that it has governed our life as

---

[39] John Rawls, *A Theory of Justice* (Cambridge, Massachusetts: Harvard University Press, 1971), pp. 60-65, 303, 404, and Part III, passim. Allan Bloom's comment on this is worth quoting:

> Rawls, because he substitutes the equal right to happiness for the equal right to life, must equalize not only the conventional primary goods but also the natural ones. The latter is harder to envisage (apart from the salutary work of geneticists who, Rawls believes, might one day improve all our progeny). One thinks of Herodotus' account of the Babylonian law by which all the marriageable girls were auctioned off; the beautiful ones brought high prices from the rich and voluptuous men; the city used the money so derived to provide dowries for the ugly girls; thus making the naturally unattractive attractive. Nature's injustice to the unendowed is what the thoroughgoing egalitarian must rectify. The redistribution of wealth is hardly sufficient, for, as we all know, the most important things are those "that money can't buy." (Allan Bloom, "Justice: John Rawls vs. the Tradition of Political Philosophy," *The American Political Science Review*, vol. 69 [June 1975], p. 654.)

[40] Alexis de Tocqueville, *Democracy in America* (New York: Vintage Books, 1945), vol. 2, p. 102.

[41] Gordon Wood, "Democracy and the Constitution," in this volume.

a people, describing the pattern of our politics, proscribing activities that in other places have prospered, and even prescribing our principles of legitimacy and illegitimacy and our understanding of political right and wrong. Its express provisions must be contended with or against, as the advocates of many a scheme or program have learned, but so must the opinions it is responsible for instilling in us. Finally, the Constitution was real to the Federalists and Antifederalists, which is why they fought so vigorously over it, and why, when it was adopted, some of them knew they had won and some of them knew they had lost.

5

Democracy and the Citizen: Community, Dignity, and the Crisis of Contemporary Politics in America

Wilson Carey McWilliams

Most Americans would agree that the Constitution has become more democratic with time.[1] We know the evidence for this view. The vote has been extended to racial minorities, women, and eighteen-year-olds. We elect senators directly, property qualifications have virtually disappeared, the poll tax is unconstitutional, and all of us are entitled to equal protection of the laws. As these examples suggest, one person, one vote is the measure by which most Americans assess degrees of democracy. Most of us, in other words, see voting by majority rule as the defining characteristic of a democratic regime.

This view is correct as far as it goes, but it rests on a fragmentary idea of democracy. I rely on an older, more comprehensive understanding that makes citizenship, rather than voting, the defining quality of democracy.[2] Common sense tells us that speaking and listening precede voting and give it form. Democracy is inseparable from democratic ways of framing and arguing for political choices. Almost all agree, for example, that elections in so-called people's democracies are shams. At a deeper level, moreover, democracy depends on those things that affect our ability to speak, hear, or be silent. In this sense, I will argue that democracy requires community, civic dignity, and religion. Similarly, I will argue that in certain important respects the Constitution, contrary to the prevailing view,

---

[1] Most political scientists probably share this view. The Constitution, Robert Dahl writes, "given the right circumstances . . . could become the government of a democratic republic. And it did." Dahl, *Pluralist Democracy in the United States* (Chicago: Rand McNally, 1967), p. 55.

[2] For similar views, see Walter Nicgorski, "The New Federalism and Direct Popular Election," *Review of Politics*, vol. 34 (1972), pp. 3-15, and Lane Davis, "The Cost of Realism: Contemporary Restatements of Democracy," *Western Political Quarterly*, vol. 17 (1964), pp. 37-46.

was more democratic in the past than it is today, especially in providing greater dignity for the citizen and greater protection against "tyranny of the majority."

My argument, obviously, extends beyond what established opinion understands by democracy, especially since my notion of democracy includes things not considered "political" by most Americans. In order to combat such deeply entrenched ways of thinking, I will have to turn to the foundations of our political thought.

The Ancient Idea of Democracy

To ancient political science, citizenship came first in the ordering of democracies. Aristotle established the first principle of democracy as political liberty, "ruling and being ruled" in turn, sharing the responsibilities of rule as well as the duty to obey.[3] In a democratic regime, each citizen must be able to share in defining the public's alternatives and have "an equal say in what is chosen and for what end."[4] Since the equality of all citizens is a democratic tenet, democracies make decisions according to number, but Aristotle took care to show that majority rule is derived from the principle of equal citizenship and shared rule.

Majority rule is, after all, a difficult precept. Why should a minority accept the rule of a majority it considers wrongheaded? According to John Locke, the authority of the majority rests on a combination of force and consent.

> It is necessary that the body should move that way whither the greater force carries it, which is the consent of the majority, or else it is impossible it should act or continue one body, one community, which the consent of every individual that united into it agreed that it should. . . .[5]

At first blush, Locke's case for majority rule rests on the minority's agreement to form a political community, but that consent as readily obliges the minority to accept *any* system of rule in preference to political dissolution or civil war. The majority's specific title derives from its "greater force"—implicitly, the impossibility, under natural conditions, of coercing the many and the ease of coercing the few. Locke, however, limited his argument to the state of nature and con-

---

[3] Ernest Barker, ed., *The Politics of Aristotle* (Oxford: Clarendon, 1952), p. 258.

[4] Delba Winthrop, "Aristotle on Participatory Democracy," *Polity*, vol. 2 (1978), p. 155.

[5] Locke, *Second Treatise on Civil Government*, sec. 96.

ditions akin to it. In civil society, as Locke knew well, majorities cannot be equated with greater force; a minority may easily comprise citizens who are wealthier and more skilled in military matters.[6] If the wealthy and strong accept the rule of the poor and unskilled, it cannot be because they are forced. It is often observed that the minority must believe that the majority will respect its "rights," ensuring its essential minimum without which it would fight. Certainly, a minority must have such confidence, but is that trust *enough?* Why would a strong minority settle for so little when force might give it so much more? The strong minority bends to majority rule only when it accepts the principle—the political equality of all citizens—from which that rule derives. I can believe that all citizens have an equal share of justice without believing that the majority is always right. You and I can be equal and ignorant when it comes to astrophysics, yet I can insist that my opinion is correct no matter how many equally ignorant people share yours.

Similarly, a strong majority refrains from oppressing the minority because it too accepts the principle of equal citizenship and political participation. The minority, as equals, must be allowed their say. (In fact, to give the minority equal time, as we do, gives it more than an equal share, since fewer citizens are allowed the same time.) As Delba Winthrop comments, a democrat who takes equal political liberty seriously "does not intend a tyranny of the majority."[7]

Both the majority and the minority must regard the principles of civic equality and equal participation more strongly than their partisan creeds and their private interests. In a democracy, citizenship rules partisanship, and public principles govern private interests. Citizens of all factions must, to that extent, prefer the good of the whole to that of the part.

Civic virtue is reemphasized by the consequences of political liberty. Aristotle observed that the democratic stress on political liberty—freedom to participate in public life as part of the whole—suggests a second form, individual liberty—"living as one likes" as though one *were* a whole. Democrats "say," Aristotle commented, that liberty must involve "living as you like," because slaves do not

---

[6] Even Locke's argument is debatable, since majorities would be particularly unlikely to have superior force in the individualistic conditions of Locke's state of nature. There is a sense in which democracy, and the virtue of majorities, does derive from force, since democracy is akin to an army. As Aristotle knew, majorities acquire force only through discipline, the ability to trust and rely on one's fellows *as a whole*, and the willingness to obey orders (provisionally at least), the reason for which we cannot see from our part of the battlefield. *The Politics of Aristotle*, pp. 182, 272, 308; Plato, *Apology*, 28d-e.

[7] Winthrop, "Aristotle on Democracy," p. 156.

live as they like.[8] This argument by democrats is evidently fallacious: "That which is not slave" is not an adequate definition of "a free person." A child who is not a slave, for example, has not come into "man's estate." This is, however, the sort of error that citizens unfamiliar with philosophy might be expected to make.

There is a second error in the democratic argument. In ordinary terms, no one lives as he "likes." The slave is not defined by living under a rule but by having no say about that rule. Voicelessness, not restraint, is the mark of a slave. This second mistake is possible only because the good citizen, in being ruled, feels he is *doing* as he likes. So he may be. The public-spirited citizen, ruling, acts for the common good; and being ruled is liberating in part since it allows a greater attention to one's own good. This is especially true if my rulers are no worse than I am, and I expect them to be guided by common principles.[9] Aristotle's argument suggests that patriotic and law-abiding but unphilosophic citizens come to believe that freedom is "living as one likes," an error that does little damage so far as they are concerned. Aristotle pointed out, however, that this idea leads to the claim of freedom from any government or, indeed, from any restraint at all. The children of public-spirited citizens, taught the mistaken "second principle" of democracy, become private-regarding individualists.[10] They may accept democracy as a second-best substitute (especially since democracy does not ask us to be ruled by anyone in particular) but it will be only that. "In this way," Aristotle observed guardedly, the second principle "contributes" to a "system of liberty based on equality."[11] Preferring to be free from all rule, the individualist supports democracy from weakness and lack of spirit, but he is not a democrat. His attitudes will be partisan or even more narrowly concerned with his own interests. If he obtains office, he will not subordinate his private will or interest to the good of the community, since to do so, in his eyes, would be slavish. Democracy can survive a few such citizens but not many. If they become predominant, majority rule will become tyrannical, with civil conflict the least danger facing the regime. The second principle, individual liberty, must be kept subordinate to the democratic first principle, political liberty and equal citizenship, if democracy is to stave off decay.

---

8 Aristotle, *Politics*, p. 258.

9 Plato, *Republic*, book 1, 346a-347d.

10 Compare Franklin's advice to Tom Paine; Benjamin Franklin, *Select Works*, P. Sargent, ed. (Boston: Phillips Sampson, 1857), p. 488.

11 Aristotle, *Politics*, p. 258.

Whatever democrats "say," democracy does not promise "living as one likes." Its aim is self-rule. Autonomy is possible for human beings only as parts of wholes, in which our "partiality" and the things to which we are "partial" are recognized as secondary, though important. In essential ways, politics frees us. In the world of the tribe, most citizens do similar work; in the city, we work at what we do best. In the clan, custom and blood-law regulate life. As a child, I am hopelessly dependent, and I value the rules of custom and kinship, which tell my parents that they must care for me. As I approach adulthood, however, this choiceless automation comes to seem impersonal, if not oppressive. The polis allows me to find friends who choose me (as I choose them) because they like me, not my genealogy.[12] In this sense, the polis is naturally "prior" to the individual, because the human being as an end presumes the polis as a means.[13]

The excellent or complete human being is the end for which the city exists; for him, if for anyone, it might be said that freedom is "doing as one likes." Such a human being, however, would recognize his debt to the city and know that his freedom involves obligations. Moreover, the most fully self-ruled men realize that the thing they rule, the self, is not something they make. My nature sets the limits to my rule. If I command myself to be young forever, my orders are hostile to self-rule, because they seek to subject the self that I am to another, imagined self. To be self-ruled, I must be ruled by my nature as a human being and by the nature of which humanity is a part. In that higher sense, self-rule does imply "doing as one likes," for it requires that I do what I truly like, according to nature, or, to put it another way, I must do what is "liked" by nature, "the one" of which I am only a part.[14]

Self-rule requires, then, that I be free to do what is according to nature. No barrier in my environment or in me must stand in the way. To help me toward self-rule, democracy must provide me with an environment that has resources enough to permit me to live in a fully human way. It must also educate me so that my soul will be free to follow nature. For its own health, democracy must try to teach me

---

[12] Because democracy emphasizes "free birth" it is more familial than its claim to freedom would suggest. Ibid., pp. 163-164. On the general point, the emphasis must be on finding friends within the city, for the friendship of all citizens is decidedly second-rate. Even though I begin by admiring what my friend appears to be, I aim at the friend I can value for what he truly is. Aristotle, *Nichomachean Ethics*, 1164a1-30, 1168a27-1169b2, and *Ethica Eudemia*, 1236a-b, 1237a-b, 1238b, 1234b.

[13] Aristotle, *Metaphysics*, 1018b9-29, discusses the varieties of "priority."

[14] Winthrop, "Aristotle on Democracy," pp. 166-167.

that human freedom is possible only when I act as a part of a whole and that my good, the good of a part, depends on that of the whole.

This lesson can never be learned perfectly. My body reminds me constantly that I am separate; my senses are my own and no one else's. The body and the senses take us beyond mere survival and pleasure; as we know, powerful feelings and passions may move us to sacrifice our lives and liberties. My body and my senses move me to such sacrifice only on behalf of things they take to be my own. The perimeter of the senses is narrow and makes me the center of the world.

When government and law urge me to support the common good, they may find an ally in my reason or my soul, but they must expect resistance from my body and my senses conducted in the name of my dignity. If, for example, reason assures me that government has consulted people like me in making policy, my emotions will answer that it has not consulted *me*.[15] Civic virtue requires that we govern some of our strongest feelings and desires. In that sense, as Aristotle argued, to rule free men—and hence, to be a citizen of a democracy—one must first learn how to be ruled.[16]

If government is radically at odds with my senses, my dignity, and my private interests, however, I will feel it as a kind of tyranny. I will resist it, retreating into private refuges if it is strong and defying it if it is weak. I may be compelled to obey, but I will not learn to be ruled.

Classical political philosophy argued in favor of the small state, in part because the *polis* was within the periphery of the senses, reducing the distance and the conflict between public good and private interest. In a small community, if my taxes help to build a reservoir, I will be drinking the water it provides and my senses will testify to benefits of civic duty. In a large state, by contrast, any benefit I derive from a dam in Idaho is indirect, as distant from my senses as Idaho itself.[17]

Similarly, the small state lets me know my fellow citizens and my rulers.[18] More important, they know *me*. This is especially true in stable communities, for people I have known only a short time are

---

[15] Peter Berger, "On the Obsolescence of the Concept of Honor," *European Journal of Sociology*, vol. 2 (1970), pp. 339-347; Anthony Lauria, "Respeto, Relajo and Interpersonal Relations in Puerto Rico," *Anthropological Quarterly*, vol. 37 (1964), pp. 53-67.

[16] Aristotle, *Politics*, p. 105.

[17] Mancur Olson, *The Logic of Collective Action* (Cambridge: Harvard University Press, 1965).

[18] Plato, *Laws*, book 5, 738e.

people I know only superficially. Moreover, if people move frequently, I will not feel confident that we share a common destiny or a common good. Rather, I am likely to suspect that they may desert me in a time of trouble; I may feel compelled to protect myself by deserting them first. The common good reigns weakly in a hobo jungle or a trailer park. Small and relatively stable communities, by contrast, encourage confidence and fidelity.

Finally, the small state is suited to democracy. In a small state, it is possible for me to have my say. In a large state, only a few can be heard beyond private circles. Small communities give a larger proportion of citizens the chance not only to speak but to speak adequately. Too, relations of trust encourage speech; we need not be silenced for fear of "giving offense" or by the suspicion that our community is too fragile to bear disagreement. Of course, a much larger percentage of the citizens of a small community can hold office. To put it another way, in the small state, I matter and my choices are visibly important. A small state comports with my dignity.[19] In this respect, it is less important that I speak or hold office than that I be able to do so. If I listen or obey, it then must be presumed that I chose to do so. Silence and law-abidingness are dignified forms of conduct. The large state, however, tends to rob obedience and silence of their dignity, making them matters of necessity. In modern America, for example, we do not really respect the respectable.

The small state is the natural home of democracy. It makes possible "ruling and being ruled in turn" and it helps to strengthen public spirit. The small state, however, demands that we restrain our ambition for power and for wealth. Similarly, democracy presumes some restraint on the extremes of wealth and poverty. Democracy does not require economic equality, but it does require a sense of commonality and equal dignity. The sense of the common good is weakened where the impoverishment of some does not affect, or even contribute to, the wealth of others. The wealthy are tempted to believe that they do not need the many and to behave with arrogance; the poor become desperate if they see their poverty as a badge of indignity and shame.[20] The desire for wealth must be restrained in all classes. Economic gain must be subordinated to stability and civility in democratic life.

In summary, democracy claims to be a regime characterized by liberty, but it depends on restraint. It requires citizens who are willing to sacrifice for the common good and, correspondingly, a restraint of

---

[19] R. E. Gehringer, "On the Moral Import of Status and Position," *Ethics*, vol. 67 (1957), pp. 200-202.

[20] Aristotle, *Politics*, pp. 63-68, 209, 232, 268.

the passions. Even those concepts that educate the passions gently, like the small state and relative economic equality, require restraint on private desires. Democracy depends on some knowledge of the limits of personal liberty and human nature. It hopes that citizens will see the law and nature not as confining prisons in which the self is trapped, but as boundaries which delineate the self. Put another way, democracy aims at the governance of body by soul. That aim is audacious. In the best of us, the body's obedience is imperfect; democracy is not a government by the best. Citizens cannot be assumed to have the faith of saints or the reason of philosophers. Democracies rely on true opinion, rather than knowledge, and on piety, rather than revelation. These lesser excellences, nevertheless, depend on the greater. Ordinary citizens need the example of the best human beings in order to imitate, as part of the exacting regimen of civic education, the reverence for law and nature which, in the best, emanates from freedom of the spirit.

The Framers' Rejection of the Ancients

Ideas like these, especially as glossed by Christian theologians, were a major part of the cultural inheritance of Americans at the birth of the Republic. Custom and controversy made many such teachings familiar to Americans who had little notion of their origins. Those who rejected classical political philosophy as a whole clung to one part or another. The framers, however, were self-consciously modern men who rejected the tradition. They felt themselves the vanguard of an intellectual revolution as well as political founders. The struggle over the form and spirit of the Constitution was, in many ways, a battle between the old science of politics and the new.

Although the framers appealed to "republican" ideals, they meant "republic" in a special, modern sense. Their real concern was liberty, not republican government, and they set as the "first object of government" the protection of the "diversity in the faculties of men." Their aim was private rather than public freedom; they elevated Aristotle's second principle to the first place in political life.[21]

Human beings, in the framers' creed, are by nature free, morally independent without obligations to nature or to their fellows. For the framers, the separateness of the body—if not the body itself—was the defining fact of human nature (hence, the tendency, in ordinary speech,

---

[21] Madison, Hamilton, and Jay, *The Federalist* Nos. 10, 39; Martin Diamond, "The Declaration and the Constitution: Liberty, Democracy and the Founders," in Nathan Glazer and Irving Kristol, eds., *The American Commonwealth 1976* (New York: Basic Books, 1975), pp. 48-49.

to separate "nature" and "nurture," equating natural conduct with what springs spontaneously from the body). By nature, our desires are free, and we seek to do as we like. Above all, we desire self-preservation, a "great principle" worthy to be ranked with "absolute necessity" and "the transcendent law of nature and of nature's God." [22]

Nature will not let us preserve ourselves. In the end, nature will kill us. The naturally free individuals of the framers' theory find themselves obstructed, at almost every point, by nature and their fellows. By nature, we strive to acquire the power to do as we will and, ultimately, to master nature itself.

By the familiar locutions of social contract theory, people discover that their unaided efforts leave them too exposed to attacks by others and too weak to trouble nature seriously. Reason suggests to the individual that he would do better in combination with others; governments are created "by the consent of the governed," since morally independent beings can be bound only by their consent. If our consent *creates* obligation, then nothing can evaluate our consent: Whatever we consent to will be "right." [23] The theory presumes, of course, that we will never truly consent to give up our rights to "life, liberty and the pursuit of happiness"; this only emphasizes that our consent (and, hence, government) can only be self-limited. As Berns demonstrates, the governed can consent, according to the Declaration of Independence, to regimes other than democracy. Civic education in an established polity does all that it need or should do when it persuades us to consent. Political participation is quite needless if we are persuaded that government protects our private rights and interests; public spirit, in any strict sense of that term, is *undesirable*. Government is always to some degree oppressive, since we give up to it some of the liberty that is ours by natural right. We ought to surrender such liberty grudgingly and watchfully; whatever civic duties our consent entails, we should perform with an eye to our private liberties. The "consent of the governed" does not require democracy, and it discourages citizenship.

For human beings as the framers understood them, the really desirable regime is not democracy, but a tyranny in which I am the tyrant, able to command the bodies and resources of others to "live as I like." Failing that, I prefer not to be ruled at all. Tyranny is unlikely and insecure, and anarchy is impractical because of the

---

[22] *Federalist* No. 43.

[23] Hanna Pitkin, "Obligation and Consent, II," *American Political Science Review*, vol. 60 (1966), pp. 39-52.

"inconveniences" of the state of nature; but these prudential objections do not affect the basic argument. Human nature strains against the law, our passions resisting the necessity to which reason gives its consent. "Why has government been instituted at all? Because the passions of men will not conform to the dictates of reason and justice without constraint." In Madison's famous rhetoric, "What is government itself but the greatest of all reflections on human nature? If men were angels, no government would be necessary," and consequently, "in framing a government . . . [y]ou must first enable the government to control the governed. . . ." [24]

In controlling the governed, majority rule—the "republican principle"—is invaluable. In the first place, all other things being equal, the majority will possess "greater force" than the minority, as in Locke's argument; its support will provide the power to constrain. Since other things are not equal, as Madison knew, and the majority is likely to be relatively poor and discontented, its consent removes one probable source of disorder.

The consent of the majority, of course, is impermanent. Having given our consent, we regret the constraint it entails, especially since under the government's protection, we forget the dangers that moved us to consent. The revolutionary war, Madison wrote, encouraged an excessive reliance on the "virtue and intelligence" of the people, since it "repressed the passions most unfriendly to order and concord," producing a patriotism not to be expected in more tranquil times. Periodic elections are needed to renew consent or, at least, to provide the government with the support of a current majority; such elections should not be so frequent as to undermine the public's "veneration" for a regime.[25] The fundamental unpolitical nature of human beings makes majority rule and periodic elections prudent, though not strictly necessary. Democracy in the modern sense derives from our supposed indisposition to all forms of rule, including democracy. The case for modern democracy rests in part on the undemocratic nature of humankind.

---

[24] *Federalist* Nos. 15, 51. Madison's implicit theology is revealing. Angels are governed, after all, by an absolute monarch, but Madison seemed to assume that the government of heaven is not relevant to earthly politics. If men were angels, Madison asserted, they would be beyond the power of nature, though not masters over it. Even with that qualification, given a modern view of the purposes of politics, no *human* government would be necessary.

[25] *Federalist* No. 49. Hegel regarded war as useful because it reminded citizens of their partiality and their need for the state (*Philosophy of Right*, part 3, pp. 320-328). Elections are a kind of "war without the knife" and hence both invaluable and dangerous.

However, majority rule and periodic elections do not oblige the government to "control itself," the second concern in framing free government. In the normal course of events, the majority will be partisan, moved by private motives, and disposed to oppression. "Neither moral nor religious motives can be relied on" to restrain it and, in any case, it is not the business of government to educate the soul. If man has a soul, it is free by nature; legitimate government is obliged to leave it so.[26]

It is no surprise then that the framers rejected the classical case for the small state. Madison was hostile to the "spirit of locality" in general, not only in the states. Small communities afford the individual less power, less mastery, and, hence, less liberty than do large states. Moreover, the small community lays hold of the affections of the individual and leads him to accept the very restraints on his interest and liberty that are inherent in smallness.[27] The classics urged the small state, in part because it might encourage the individual to limit and rule his private passions. Madison rejected such states, because he rejected that sort of restraint. Small communities limit opportunities and meddle with the soul. At best, they are outdated associations that once advanced individual interests but now fetter the new science of politics.

All "face-to-face" communities are suspect. In very small districts, Madison warned, representatives are likely to be "unduly attached" to their constituents. The affections are too intense, the bonds of community too strong. "Great and national objects" on one hand, and individual liberty on the other, are necessarily endangered. In a large assembly, especially if it is "changeable," the individual is not attached *enough*. In the crowd, the individual is too anonymous for a "sensible degree of praise or blame for public measures" to attach to him. His private passions are loosed because he is freed from the consequences of his acts. At the same time, by the face-to-face quality of the assembly, the individual is enabled to discover those who share his ambitions, resentments, and desires. "A common passion or interest will, in almost every case, be felt by a majority of the whole; a communication and concert results from the form of government itself. . . ."[28]

In one context, Madison seemed to suggest that the problem results from our unequal capacities for reason.

---

[26] *Federalist* Nos. 51, 10.

[27] Julian Boyd, ed., *The Papers of Thomas Jefferson* (Princeton: Princeton University Press, 1950-), vol. 6, pp. 308-309.

[28] *Federalist* Nos. 10, 63.

> In a nation of philosophers. . . . [a] reverence for the laws would be sufficiently inculcated by the voice of an enlightened reason. But a nation of philosophers is as little to be expected as the philosophical race of kings wished for by Plato.[29]

In fact, however, a nation of philosophers would make no difference if it were a polis: "Had every Athenian citizen been a Socrates; every Athenian assembly would still have been a mob." [30] This is a striking, even shocking, assertion, although it follows from the framers' theory. Madison argued that the passions can never be educated, even in the best and wisest human beings; they can only be repressed and controlled. In the assembly, each citizen-Socrates would sense his anonymity. He would no longer fear the shame of visibly pursuing private interests or oppressive designs, and he would join others in carrying these designs into effect. Socrates is not king, "the epitome of a free man who participates in politics for the common good" and a model for democratic citizens, but a craven tyrant who fears being found out.[31]

If this is true of Socrates, it is even more true of the rest of us. There are no citizens in the classical sense of the term, just as there are no kings. There are only tyrants, more or less strong. Liberty requires that we be kept weak. The small state, however, makes us feel strong or, at least, that we matter. That very virtue, in the framers' eyes, becomes a damning vice.

Madison and Hamilton argued that the control of the majority lies in the "enlargement of the orbit" of republican rule, creating a large state in which a majority must be composed of diverse factions, unlikely to agree about much or for long. The number of such factions, however, is no more important than the distance between the bodies of the individuals composing the factions. That distance guarantees that a common sentiment cannot be felt, except in so diffuse a form as to be unimportant. The ideal regime is "dispassionate" even more than "disinterested." Interest, at least, is calculable and easily channeled by institutions and laws. The passions must be "controlled and regulated" by government.[32]

Free government aims to minimize coercion, but the passions can be disciplined without much direct force. Human beings will be fearful enough when they are weak and alone.

---

[29] *Federalist* No. 49.

[30] *Federalist* No. 55.

[31] Winthrop, "Aristotle on Democracy," p. 166.

[32] Robert Rutland et al., eds., *The Papers of James Madison* (Chicago: University of Chicago Press, 1962-), vol. 9, p. 384; *Federalist* No. 49.

The reason of man, like man himself, is timid and cautious when left alone; and acquires firmness and confidence, in proportion to the number with which it is associated.[33]

Individuals in the large state, unable to "communicate and concert" easily, are likely to feel "timid and cautious." The states and local communities, however, are barriers to this salutary isolation. In them, individuals are too intimately associated with others who are close to their affections; citizens are encouraged to be rash and turbulent in relation to the general government, while local regimes deprive them of private liberty. Consequently, the federal government must gain direct access to the individual, breaking the locality's monopoly on his affections and attracting to the central regime "those passions which have the strongest influence upon the human heart."[34] At least somewhat freed from local regimes, the individual will also be more timid, cautious, and alone.

This has a benefit beyond fearful obedience. Since human reason "acquires firmness and confidence in proportion to the number with which it is associated," those opinions shared by the majority of Americans will be held with overwhelming force. There will not be many such opinions—no more, perhaps, than the general principles of the Declaration of Independence—but they will be all but unquestioned. In the large state, weak individuals hesitate to advance eccentric views and adopt with confidence ideas shared by the many. It is a strange result for a theory that began with a concern for the freedom of the soul.

The Antifederalists and the Old Science of Politics

However, as Young reminds us, the framers did not have it all their own way. We tend, in fact, to underestimate the strength of Antifederalist views, since many who shared Antifederalist beliefs and apprehensions joined Jefferson in accepting the Constitution as a working document, hoping to shape it by interpretation, practice, and amendment.[35] The federalism of the Constitution resulted from politics, not from the framers' wishes. Both Madison and Hamilton desired a far more centralized regime than that framed in the Constitution.[36]

---

[33] *Federalist* No. 49.

[34] *Federalist* No. 16.

[35] Adrienne Koch and William Peden, eds., *The Life and Selected Writings of Thomas Jefferson* (New York: Modern Library, 1944), p. 441.

[36] Gaillard Hunt, ed., *The Writings of James Madison* (New York: Putnam, 1900-1910), vol. 2, pp. 336-340; Max Farrand, ed., *The Records of the Federal Convention* (New Haven: Yale University Press, 1937), vol. 1, pp. 162, 164, 168, 297, 463-464, 476, 489-490, 530; vol. 2, pp. 390-391; vol. 3, p. 77.

While the Antifederalists, as Berns comments, spoke in the language of rights and contracts then current among educated men, their position derived from the older science of politics. The language of individual rights did not really suit the Antifederalists. They were far more likely than their antagonists to refer to government and society as "natural." Civic virtue was a central concern of their political argument, and they were zealous to defend true opinion and small states as the foundations of civic education. Centinel scorned governments that were republican in "form" only, insisting that the "reality" required a virtuous people. As Berns observes, Antifederalists sometimes supported religious tests and, even more often, legislation to promote public morals. A free people, Melancton Smith argued, is necessarily exposed by its very freedom to a "fickle and inconstant" spirit. Government must be vulnerable to this inconstancy. Free government requires the foundation provided by a stable private order, the "old communities" settled in "time and habit" to which Samuel Bryan appealed. Such communities should be rooted in the people's affections. They require an ordered life and a rough equality, protecting community against the conflicts engendered by luxury, competition, and anxiety. A democracy, George Clinton said in a nice turn of phrase, should be "well-digested." [37]

Only in small states, Richard Henry Lee contended, can the laws possess the "confidence" of the people. Confidence, we should remember, is a much more active and embracing term than "consent." It suggests speaking one's mind, as in "confiding" to another. It also implies that citizens "confide"—give or entrust—themselves to the laws, yielding private interest and opinion to public rule. Such a spirit required, Lee observed, a government within the emotional, sensory range of the individual, one limited like man himself, Agrippa wrote, to a "narrow space." [38]

A federal regime could acquire confidence only if representatives, who make the laws, are able to convey it. In the first place, the citizen must know his representative and be known by him, establishing a tie between the "natural aristocracy" and the "democracy." No "government of strangers" is acceptable.[39] For Madison, it was enough that the representative know the "local circumstances and lesser interests" of the electors. George Mason argued, by contrast, that the representative should "mix with the people, think as they think,

---

[37] Cecilia Kenyon, ed., *The Antifederalists* (Indianapolis: Bobbs-Merrill, 1966), pp. xcii, 148, 197, 205, 263, 309-310, 374, 388.

[38] Ibid., pp. 154, 210.

[39] Ibid., pp. lxi, 216-217, 377-378, 383-385.

feel as they feel—ought to be perfectly amenable to them and thoroughly acquainted with their interest and condition."[40] Mason included Madison's demand for an intellectual knowledge of the "interest and condition" of the people, but he put it last, giving precedence to the requirement of emotional comprehension and personal relationship, considerations Madison put aside.

Moreover, if the representative is to convey confidence, he must represent the minority as well as the majority. For this to be possible, majorities and minorities, like the citizens Aristotle described, must prefer the public good to their partisan interests. The district must be a community, convinced that its likenesses outweigh its differences.

To Madison's objection—that very small districts tie representatives to parochial interests—the Antifederalists responded that only such districts can give the representative the authority (confidence) to *sacrifice* private interests. Of course, representatives from small districts may be mean or private-spirited. Unless the electors are ensured their say, however, they will not consider themselves represented and, resenting the indignity, they will stand on the defensive. In a large district, we may trust our representative to defend the district's interests; we are unlikely to trust his decision to sacrifice them.[41]

Madison's argument illustrates his differences with the Antifederalists. The district must be large enough to avoid "undue attachment," but small enough for the representative to know the district's interest. This latter limit, however, is not a strict one. A shrewd representative can master the interests of a large district. Congressmen today, who represent close to a half million people, prove the point. In fact, if a district is large, according to Madison's principles, it should be very large, since in all face-to-face meetings, passion prevails. On the other hand, a "numerous and changeable" body cannot be moved by a sense of the common good.[42] This comment, in relation to the Senate, illuminates Madison's intent. Congressional districts, intended to be large if not especially changeable, are not *meant* to be moved by the common good. The refusal of a minority within such districts to be "represented" merely adds another faction to the multiplicity that protects liberty, and it may help to fragment locality. Madison rejected a system of representation intended to convey confidence, public-spirited support for the common good, in favor of representatives who can provide the consent of a "numerous and changeable" multifactional majority.

[40] *Federalist* No. 10; Kenyon, p. lii.
[41] Paul L. Ford, *Essays on the Constitution of the United States, 1787-1788* (Brooklyn: Historical Printing Club, 1892), p. 73; Kenyon, pp. 310-312.
[42] *Federalist* No. 63.

Madison also maintained that large districts would be more likely to contain "fit characters" than small ones. Since candidates would be less able, in large districts, to practice the "vicious arts" of electioneering, "fit characters" would be more likely to win office. Madison, of course, knew well that demagogy is easier when addressing a large audience than a small one; that is not the sort of "vicious art" he had in mind. He referred to "cabals" that organized (and often bribed) local electorates. Organizing or bribing a large electorate is undeniably more difficult; hence, the "suffrages of the people" would be more "free." As a result, well-known and celebrated persons would be more likely to win election.[43]

This argument, however, illustrates what John Lansing meant when he observed that elections can be only the "form" of freedom.[44] All elections require some organization; the selection of contending candidates and the identification of "serious" contenders in a large field are obvious examples. Large electorates favor those with established advantages—the wealthy, the famous, and urbanites, who "live compact" with "constant connection and intercourse."[45] The Antifederalists, on the whole, were partisans of direct election, but, unlike later and less wise enthusiasts, they recognized that mass electorates are to the advantage of *elites*. Martin Van Buren observed thirty-five years later that nonpartisan elections benefit the upper classes and the celebrated and consequently undermine respect for institutions by inspiring the belief that elections are a fraud, concealing "real" decisions made elsewhere.[46] To the Antifederalists, democratic elections were tied to the local polls, closer to a caucus than to the secret ballot and relatively open to the candidacy of ordinary citizens. The Antifederalists retained the idea of a citizen as someone who shares in rule, hence their support for annual elections and rotation in office. All citizens, George Clinton declared, should have the chance to win public office and honor, for the "desire of rendering themselves worthy" of office nurtures patriotism and civic virtue.[47] In this, too,

---

[43] *Federalist* No. 10.

[44] Jonathan Elliot, *Debates in the Several State Conventions on the Adoption of the Federal Constitution* (Philadelphia: Lippincott, 1896), vol. 2, p. 295; Kenyon, p. 72.

[45] Kenyon, *Antifederalists*, p. liv; James Madison, in A. Koch, ed., *Notes of Debates in the Federal Convention of 1787* (Athens: Ohio University Press, 1966), pp. 235, 194.

[46] James Ceasar, "Political Parties and Presidential Ambition," *Journal of Politics*, vol. 40 (1978), pp. 725, 728.

[47] Kenyon, *Antifederalists*, pp. 310-311; Elliot, *Debates on Adoption of the Constitution*, vol. 2, p. 295.

the Antifederalists defended the older science of politics against the new.

Trained in a rhetoric that exaggerated dangers in order to anticipate them, the Antifederalists overstated the immediacy of the threat posed by the Constitution.[48] They were sometimes wrong altogether about specific provisions. In the main, however, they understood the Constitution correctly. "Consolidation," the Pennsylvania Antifederalists observed, "pervades the whole document."[49] The states, close to the people, possessed their confidence and affection and were safe against direct assault. The shrewd reader, however, would discern a "certain . . . studied ambiguity" in the language of the Constitution, made more ominous with all "essential" powers given to the central government.[50] Antifederalists were not mollified by reassurances: "It is a mere fallacy, invented by the deceptive powers of Mr. Wilson, that what rights are not given are reserved."[51] In the combination of power and ambiguity, the Antifederalists detected a desire to reduce the states, "slowly and imperceptibly," to a "shadow of power," forms without functions.[52] It would be hard, in the event, to argue that the Antifederalists did not read the Constitution properly.

Established opinion, especially attachment to states and localities, imposed on the framers. By its influence on politics and political men, the older idea of democracy voiced by the Antifederalists profoundly affected the use and interpretation of the Constitution and its powers. In many ways, American political history can be read as a conflict between the institutional design of the Constitution, reflecting the framers' "new science," and public mores, habits, and beliefs. Alexis de Tocqueville gave his opinion that the "manners of the Americans" were the "real cause" of our ability to maintain democratic government.[53] However, George Clinton was correct: "Opinion and manners are mutable," especially given the "progress of commercial society"; in the long run, the government "assimilates the manners and opinions of the community to it."[54] Clinton's observation suggests an amendment to Tocqueville: The manners of the Americans are more impor-

---

[48] On the rhetoric of the Antifederalists and its origins, see Kenyon, p. xlv, and Harvey Mansfield, Jr., *The Spirit of Liberalism* (Cambridge: Harvard University Press, 1978), pp. 79-80.

[49] Kenyon, *Antifederalists*, p. 45.

[50] Ibid., pp. lxxv, 212-213.

[51] Ibid., p. 141.

[52] Ibid., pp. 265, 212-213, 43, 127.

[53] Alexis de Tocqueville, *Democracy in America* (New York: Schocken, 1961), vol. 1, p. 383.

[54] Kenyon, *Antifederalists*, pp. 308-309.

tant than the laws, but, in the end, the laws transform manners in their own image.

Certainly, that is what the framers hoped. Thwarted of his centralizing ambitions, Madison became, with years, more tolerant of the states. He had not changed his aims. He simply became more convinced that indirect means, flowing especially from the power of commerce, would achieve his goal. The railroads, he told George Bancroft, would "dovetail" the states. (Justice Johnson, concurring in *Gibbons* v. *Ogden*, similarly observed that with the "advancement of society," commerce necessarily comes to include more and more spheres of life.) [55] The new science of politics was too subtle to attempt frontal attacks; the older traditions, lacking the clarity and coherence of the classical science of politics from which they derived, were too easily confused to do more than fight a stubborn delaying action. The older idea of democracy now faces final defeat, and its defenders seem reduced to garbled romanticism. The triumph of the new democracy over the old, however, is a bleak enough prospect to alarm any surviving citizens into wakefulness.

The Framers' Triumph and Tyranny of the Majority

Fifty years after the ratification of the Constitution, Tocqueville refined and restated the Antifederalist case. In large states, Tocqueville argued, democracy was especially exposed to "tyranny of the majority." Equality denies the authority of one individual over another, but it suggests the authority of the many over the few. When society is small enough so that the majority may be perceived as *individuals*, equality permits and encourages me to discount it. Consequently, "small nations have therefore ever been the cradle of political liberty." Tocqueville, in fact, seemed to reverse the framers' argument: The instability and turbulence of small states is the mark of their freedom, the proof that local tyrannies, however intrusive, can be overthrown. Tocqueville referred to political, not individual, liberty. The small state's limited resources check individual ambition and direct the citizen to the cultivation of the "internal benefit of the community," including the nurturing of civic virtue. Large states are better suited to great projects and the pursuit of power, particularly because, unlike localities, they are rarely governed by custom. [56] Large

[55] Madison's comment is related in Bancroft's biography, *Martin Van Buren* (New York: Harper and Bros., 1889). Justice Johnson's comments are only a little more explicit than Marshall's opinion for the Court (Gibbons v. Ogden, 9 Wheat. 1, 1824).

[56] Tocqueville, *Democracy in America*, vol. 1, pp. 176-177, 179.

states, then, may suit private liberty, but large *democracies* are a particular case.

Given the weight of numbers, the idea of equality makes it hard for me, even in spirit, to oppose the majority. The majority becomes overwhelming, impersonal, and imponderable. I cannot perceive it as so many faces, since it has become faceless. In the small state, I may hope to change enough votes by my eloquence or my skill at electioneering to transform a minority into a majority. In large states, such a result is improbable at best. The "tyranny of the majority" was not like the coherent majority factions which Madison feared, nor was it like the tyrannies of the past. It was an "affair of the mind," crushing the spirit as it left the body free. Later in the century, James Bryce referred to the "fatalism of the multitude," contending that most Americans, taking their impotence for granted, regarded prevailing opinions as "facts of nature" to which they could only adapt. In such circumstances, public criticism of dominant ideas would be rare, hesitant, probably ignored and, in the end, likely to be forgotten.[57]

Along with this tendency to public conformity, Tocqueville observed, went an inclination to private self-seeking and "individualism." Making the citizen feel insignificant, mass democracy affronts his dignity, losing most of its chance to nurture civic virtue. Public life injures the citizen's self-esteem, and he retreats into private life, especially when established opinion speaks of the right to, and the rightness of, private liberty. As the public sphere grows larger and more powerful, the private sphere shrinks, the individual breaking his ties to his fellows one after another, a "freedom" which "threatens in the end to confine him entirely within the solitude of his own heart."[58]

This combination of public freedom and private weakness, with its attendant consequence, nearly uniform adherence to those ideas supported by large majorities, is precisely what Madison had urged and sought to establish. Seeking to avoid the despotism of a visible majority, the framers had encouraged the tyranny of an invisible one. Freeing the body, they had made it too easy to enslave the soul.

Tocqueville saw several barriers to tyranny of the majority. Religion taught Americans a law beyond the will of the majority and a code of morals at odds with calculations of utility. It commanded love and sacrifice, the moral signs of nobility. Divine monarchy restrained and elevated secular democracy, especially since the loneliest Ameri-

---

[57] Ibid., vol. 1, pp. 298-318. James Bryce, *The American Commonwealth* (New York: Commonwealth, 1908), vol. 2, pp. 358-368.

[58] Tocqueville, *Democracy in America*, vol. 2, pp. 118-120.

can could seek asylum from the tyranny of the majority at the feet of the king.[59]

Second, local regimes appealed to the citizen's dignity and "engendered and nurtured" his civic spirit. "The public spirit of the Union is . . . nothing more than an abstract of the patriotic zeal of the provinces." [60] Finally, local regimes enabled the citizen to learn the "arts of association" through participation, making him stronger and more confident in relation to national majorities. Public life became a source of dignity rather than humiliation. Without politics, an American "would be robbed of one half of his existence. He would feel an immense void in the life which he is accustomed to lead, and his wretchedness would be unbearable." [61]

Tocqueville did not highly value American political parties, but clearly they belong in his case. Many a Republican is able to defy majority opinions because he can identify them as Democratic heresies. Rooted in local ward and precinct allegiances, traditional parties—by a hierarchy of personal relationships and partisan fraternities—connected the "right opinion" of localities to the national regime. Similarly, parties appealed to private motives (the desire for jobs and honors, loyalty to one's friends, and hatred for one's enemies), hoping to woo them to the support of public principles and honor. Traditional parties were, in crucial ways, the schools for civic education, inculcating the middling sort of civic virtue possible in a vast state.[62]

Today, however, all these institutions are in disarray. Religion is in retreat; the evangelical exceptions to the rule, far from denying the general tendency, proclaim it fervently. Increasingly, states and localities lack the resources needed to address public problems. Ignore the effects of war; commerce alone has devoured the local community and reduced local regimes to near impotence. The Supreme Court conceded long ago that commerce, "the plainest facts of our national life," must take precedence over federalism in defining the constitutional order.[63] The Court's decision was probably prudent, but the ascendancy of economic life over locality implies the supremacy of private motives, pursued in accord with presumed "necessities," over

---

[59] Ibid., vol. 1, pp. 355-373; vol. 2, pp. 22-32, 170-177.

[60] Ibid., vol. 1, p. 181.

[61] Ibid., vol. 1, p. 293; see also vol. 1, pp. 216-226, 331-339.

[62] I make a similar argument in "Political Parties as Civic Associations," in Gerald Pomper, ed., *Party Renewal in America* (New York: Praeger, 1980), pp. 51-68.

[63] National Labor Relations Board v. Jones and Laughlin, 301 U.S. 1 (1937).

deliberation and choice. That, obviously, is not good news for democracy.

The states and localities have lost more than material power; their influence on our characters and their hold on our affections are rapidly declining. Localities are decreasingly stable (approximately a quarter of the population moves every year); trust is necessarily limited and superficial.[64] More and more, we live in neighborhoods and social circles that are not political bodies combining all or most of the things necessary for the good life, but associations formed on the basis of highly specialized similarities of private pursuit and fortune.[65] Too much of what we need and are is left out of such "communities" for us to confide much of ourselves to them. We live increasingly private lives, as Tocqueville warned; instability and weakness erode our capacities for intimacy, life beyond the moment, and mutual dependence. Even the family is embattled, rivaled by the impermanent relationships it is coming to resemble. The "culture of narcissism" bespeaks the fall of the great barriers to tyranny of the majority.[66]

In public and economic life, the citizen is dwarfed by titanic organizations and confused by change. Inequalities of wealth and position are only a part of the problem, though such inequalities undoubtedly restrict access to office or to the rostrum. Those social critics who suggest that capitalism and private wealth are the root of all the ills of American democracy are guilty of making our problems appear less severe than they are. Wealth *can* be limited or equalized, although assembling a majority to support such policies would be difficult. Inequalities of organizational power are less tractable. Large-scale organizations are an artifact of the size and complexity of our regime. Any organization large enough to affect the market or the government's policy is almost certain to be so large as to offend the dignity of its members. We can regulate these private regimes but only by increasing *public* bureaucracy and large-scale organization.[67]

The mass media are prototypic of such "private governments." In one sense, the media control who is allowed to address the public and on what terms. Private, often self-selected, leaders in the media

[64] See my essay, "American Pluralism: the Old Order Passeth," in Irving Kristol and Paul Weaver, eds., *The Americans, 1976* (Lexington: Heath, 1976), pp. 293-320.

[65] John H. Schaar, "Equality of Opportunity and Beyond," in Roland Pennock and John W. Chapman, eds., *Equality* (New York: Atherton, 1967), pp. 228-249.

[66] Christopher Lasch, *The Culture of Narcissism* (New York: Norton, 1979) and *Haven in a Heartless World* (New York: Basic Books, 1977).

[67] Grant McConnell, *Private Power and American Democracy* (New York: Knopf, 1966).

chair our public forum, able to set the terms of deliberation.[68] Sponsors, at least in television, have little control over content; a program with a strong following finds a seller's market. *Both* sponsors and media leaders are dominated by their eagerness for programs that score well in the "ratings." Our choice of programs, however, is no democratic decision. When we turn the dial, we do not make a decision which consciously involves *public* standards. (This matters. Not long ago, a majority endorsed the idea of "family time" as public policy while expressing distaste for the programs that filled such slots.) We certainly do not deliberate. The "ratings" aggregate our private choices, and those choices, in turn, tyrannize the media's "men of power." At the same time, a host of specialized journals and radio stations appeals to narrowing private circles. The public sphere expands, the private sphere contracts. Neither speaks the language of citizenship or democracy.

The citizen finds little in public life to elevate his spirit or support his dignity; he finds much that damages both. Political parties, which sought to connect private feelings with public life, are waning along with the communities that were their foundation.[69] Increasingly, the citizen retreats into the "solitude of his own heart," denying the country the allegiance it needs to address looming crises and himself those possibilities that still exist for friendship and freedom.

Democracy has few footholds in modern America. Strengthening democratic life is a difficult, even daunting, task requiring sacrifice and patience more than dazzling exploits. Foreign policy alone forbids dismantling the mass state. We could equalize wealth but not power. Wealth—to the extent that it differs from organizational power—at least complicates the lives of our organizational oligarchs. Even if, by some miracle, we *could* equalize power and make all Americans equal in all things, we would still face the stubborn problem of dignity. In the mass state, indignity is inherent. In such a state, equality would imply that *no one* matters. I have no desire to minimize the grievances of the poor, but it seems to me that indignity, not inequality, is our real complaint. A great many Americans would forgo material gains if they felt they were listened to or even that their *listening* mattered. A great many more would make greater sacrifices if they felt they would be known and remembered.

Democratic citizenship requires dignity. Neither dignity nor citizenship is at home in an unstable society or a large state. Whatever

[68] Bertrand de Jouvenel, "The Chairman's Problem," *American Political Science Review*, vol. 55 (1961), pp. 368-372.

[69] Gerald M. Pomper, "The Decline of the Party in American Elections," *Political Science Quarterly*, vol. 92 (1977), pp. 21-41.

possibilities we have for democratic life require us to turn government's resources to the task of protecting and reconstructing local community and private order. We can, at least, repeal laws that place families at a disadvantage in taxation, that weaken local communities, and that are designed to shatter political parties. We can seek laws and policies that enhance and support stability in our relationships, our expectations, and our laws themselves. A "transformation" is required only in a very special sense; we need a movement away from the transformations that have regularly weakened the democratic aspects of our life.

Democracy requires, I think, an end to the moral dominion of the great modern project that set humankind in pursuit of the mastery of nature. Democracy is for friends and citizens, not masters and slaves. The ultimate ground for democratic ideas of equality and the highest limitation on democracy's excesses both derive from a universe in which humanity is at home, my dignity is guaranteed by the majesty of the law I obey, and perhaps even "those who have no memorial" do not pass from memory.

6

Deliberative Democracy: The Majority Principle in Republican Government

Joseph M. Bessette

Virtually all the disagreement and confusion about the democratic character of the Constitution stem from one indisputable fact: its framers defended it as simultaneously an embodiment of majority rule and an institutional mechanism which embraced various salutary restraints on the majority. On the one hand, the Constitution was nothing less than "strictly republican," and it was the "fundamental maxim of republican government . . . that the sense of the majority should prevail."[1] On the other hand, this same Constitution created a bicameral legislature, an independent presidential office with a qualified veto over legislative acts, and a Supreme Court whose members held office for life (barring impeachment)—all defended as necessary for the government to resist unwise or unjust popular inclinations.[2] How, then, can we make sense of this apparent contradiction? There are two broad possibilities. Either the framers engaged in deception, employing democratic rhetoric to defend a less than democratic document, or they shared an understanding of majority rule according to which *certain* kinds of restraints on the popular will did not violate the basic principle itself.

It is probably fair to say that since the Progressive Era the dominant view among scholars in this country, certainly among the most influential American historians, has been the former. From J. Allen Smith and Charles Beard to the present, interpreters have made much of the Constitution's "checks" on popular majorities, but little of the framers' repeated assertions that they were the true friends of popular government and that their institutional scheme held

---

[1] Alexander Hamilton, James Madison, and John Jay, *The Federalist Papers*, ed. Clinton Rossiter (New York: New American Library, 1961), No. 39, p. 240; No. 22, p. 146.

[2] Ibid., No. 63, p. 384; No. 71, p. 432; and No. 78, pp. 469-70.

out far brighter prospect of effective majority rule than the seemingly more democratic proposals of their opponents (proposals, for example, to preserve the ascendancy of the states in the federal system because these were "closer to the people" than the national government).

The most impressive recent contribution to this view is Gordon Wood's *The Creation of the American Republic, 1776-1787*.[3] Drawing upon a detailed analysis of the political writings of the founding period, Wood maintains that "the quarrel [over the Constitution] was fundamentally one between aristocracy and democracy."[4] In opposing the new Constitution, the Antifederalists defended the rise of the "middling and lower classes of people" to positions of political power in the revolutionary period, especially in the states. The Federalists, however, saw this as the main cause of social disorder and political instability. They sought through their new institutions to promote the rule of the "natural aristocracy," by which they meant the elite social class from which they came and which had dominated colonial politics. Hence, "the Constitution was an intrinsically aristocratic document designed to check the democratic tendencies of the period."[5] The framers used "the most popular and democratic rhetoric available to explain and justify their aristocratic system."[6]

A similar argument about the framers' intentions, which is part of a larger critique of the American political system, is advanced by Michael Parenti in *Democracy for the Few*.[7] Parenti, however, goes further than Wood in emphasizing the concrete material motives of the framers. Representing a cross section of the nation's propertied interests, the framers feared the threat which growing democratization posed for their social position and economic livelihood. Consequently, they designed a new set of institutions that would *"fragment power without democratizing it."*[8] Through the familiar devices of separation of powers and checks and balances, "they hoped to dilute the impact of popular sentiments."[9] Indeed, "their uppermost concern was to diminish popular control."[10] Hence, the Constitution "was and still is largely an elitist document."[11] Whether one calls it "aris-

---

[3] Gordon Wood, *The Creation of the American Republic, 1776-1787* (New York: W. W. Norton, 1972). See also his essay in this volume.

[4] Ibid., p. 485.

[5] Ibid., p. 513.

[6] Ibid., p. 562.

[7] Michael Parenti, *Democracy for the Few*, 2d ed. (New York: St. Martin's Press, 1977), chap. 4, pp. 49-62. See also his essay in this volume.

[8] Ibid., p. 56. Emphasis in original.

[9] Ibid.

[10] Ibid., p. 60.

[11] Ibid.

tocratic" or "elitist," the point is the same: the Constitution was designed to promote the power and values of the "few" over that of the "many."

There can be no dispute that the framers desired to place certain kinds of restraints on certain kinds of popular majorities. Reading their works in this more democratic age, one is continually struck by the framers' directness and forthrightness in explaining to the people why popular inclinations must sometimes be resisted by those who govern. (The contrast with President Carter, who repeatedly and publicly proclaimed his desire to make the government as good as the people, could hardly be sharper.) It was precisely the framers' unwillingness to obscure or finesse this issue, this principle of their system, that has gotten them into trouble with more recent interpreters. The framers have been taken at their word, but only part of their message has been accepted. This was less true at the time of the ratification struggle itself. The success of the framers' proposal before democratically elected state conventions is evidence that among the American people in 1787–1789 the two sides of the framers' argument—the need to restrain popular majorities but also to effectuate majority rule—were not seen as incompatible. It is the thesis of this essay that the key to the reconciliation of these apparently contradictory intentions lies in the framers' broad purpose to establish a "deliberative democracy."

Government through Representatives

As is well known, the framers rejected "simple" or "pure" democracy as the proper model for the new American government. In a pure democracy, the people actually meet together and make binding political decisions on the most important matters facing the state. Obviously, such a scheme of government was rendered impossible by the size and population of the American nation (although modern technologies like two-way television have now made something like direct democracy technically feasible). For the framers, however, the unsuitability of direct democracy went deeper than its impracticality. History had demonstrated that democracies were continually subject to tumult, disorder, and confusion; that citizens often sacrificed their independent judgment to the pleasing promises of artful orators; and that the rights of minorities (whether economic, religious, or ethnic) were regularly violated by tyrannical majorities. These defects were endemic to pure democracies, whatever their particular historical, cultural, or social conditions.

This record taught the framers not that majority rule was doomed to failure, leaving as viable alternatives only rule by the "one" or the "few," but rather that the majority must be made to rule *through representatives*. This would have two benefits. First, it would allow one government to extend over a much larger population and territory, thereby making it more difficult for an unjust majority to come together and execute its designs. Second, it would

> refine and enlarge the public views by passing them through the medium of a chosen body of citizens, whose wisdom may best discern the true interest of their country and whose patriotism and love of justice will be least likely to sacrifice it to temporary or partial considerations. Under such a regulation it may well happen that the public voice, pronounced by the representatives of the people, will be more consonant to the public good than if pronounced by the people themselves, convened for the purpose.[12]

This quotation from James Madison's famous tenth *Federalist* essay contains the germ of the notion of "deliberative democracy," which is given fuller expression in later numbers of *The Federalist*. The essential point is that through the operation of the representative principle "public views" are "refine[d] and enlarge[d]"; they are not simply displaced by the personal views of the representatives. What results can be called "the public voice," although it is not pronounced by the people directly. What, however, is the meaning of such a description for the decisions of legislators if these differ in important respects from the direct desires of the people themselves? We seem to have two "public voice[s]."

To make sense of this requires a consideration of why representatives can be expected to make better laws than the people directly. First, they are generally more knowledgeable and experienced than their constituents. Second, they operate in an environment that fosters collective reasoning about common concerns, while their constituents usually lack the time, inclination, or setting to engage in a similar enterprise. Neither point implies any failing on the part of the citizenry; it is wholly unrealistic to expect people who spend most of their time earning a living to match the effort devoted by the legislator to public issues. Nor do these points necessarily lead to undemocratic results, that is, to laws that violate the will of the majority. The hypothetical test would be something like the following. If the citizens possessed the same knowledge and experience as their representatives and if they devoted the same amount of time

---

[12] *Federalist* No. 10, p. 82.

reasoning about the relevant information and arguments presented in the legislative body, would they reach fundamentally similar conclusions on public policy issues as their representatives? If the answer is yes, then we must conclude that the result is basically democratic, even though the outcome may differ substantially from the citizens' *original* inclinations or desires. When confronted by a public opinion pollster, for example, an individual may voice approval for any number of noble sounding legislative initiatives, but such support may dissolve upon the simple consideration of matters like cost and feasibility.

There are, then, two kinds of majority sentiments, two types of public voice. The one is more immediate or spontaneous, uninformed, and unreflective; the other is more deliberative, taking longer to develop and resting on a fuller consideration of information and arguments. It is the second type that the framers sought to promote; this is what they meant when they talked about the rule of the majority. In the service of this end, the rule of the *deliberative majority*, political leaders were obliged to resist, at least for a time, unreflective popular sentiments that were unwise or unjust:

> When occasions present themselves in which the interests of the people are at variance with their inclinations, it is the duty of the persons whom they have appointed to be the guardians of those interests to withstand the temporary delusion in order to give them time and opportunity for more cool and sedate reflection.[13]

In the framers' view, these short-term checks on unsound popular inclinations did not violate majority rule properly understood, that is, the rule of the deliberative majority. Indeed, such checks were absolutely essential to the formation, expression, and effective political rule of informed and reasoned majority judgments. The task of the republican constitution maker was to fashion a set of institutions that would strike just the right balance between responsiveness and restraint, that would foster the rule of the deliberative majority by protecting it against the dangers of unreflective popular sentiments.

The Deliberative Sense of the Community

It remains true, of course, that under the Constitution actual political decisions are made by elected officials, not by the majority directly, regardless of how deliberative. This opens the possibility that governmental decisions may reflect more the personal views of political

---

13 Ibid., No. 71, p. 432.

leaders than the considered judgments of the people. This problem cannot be ignored under any arrangement that excludes direct popular influence in the government. Nonetheless, the framers believed that in the new American government deliberative majority sentiment would prevail. Both Madison and Alexander Hamilton made the point explicitly. In discussing the Senate the former held that "the cool and deliberate sense of the community ought, in all governments, and actually will, in all free governments, ultimately prevail over the views of its rulers."[14] Hamilton used similar language in discussing the presidency: "The republican principle demands that the deliberate sense of the community should govern the conduct of those to whom they intrust the management of their affairs."[15]

If these are accurate characterizations of the American political system, if our fundamental law does make "the deliberate sense of the community" the effective ruling force, then the charge that the Constitution is an "aristocratic" or "elitist" document cannot stand. To assess the soundness of the framers' argument two questions must be addressed. First, given the specific features of the framers' institutional design, was theirs a reasonable expectation? Second, does the historical record generally support their contention?

When the framers rejected direct popular participation in the governing process, they put their faith instead in political institutions. It was their hope that these institutions would in effect actualize the deliberative sense of the community. On most issues the citizenry would do its reasoning through its representatives. The representatives, then, must share the basic values and goals of their constituents; their own deliberations about public policy must be firmly rooted in popular interests and inclinations. This is ensured through an electoral scheme that provides for periodic accountability to the public of the members of each of the political branches. In the initial elections the public can be expected to select for its rulers individuals sympathetic to their desires; in the reelection contests the public will judge the records of incumbents against the promises of their challengers.

Different degrees of accountability apply for members of the House and Senate and for the presidency. With popular election and two-year terms, members of the House were most directly answerable to the public. Members of the Senate, on the other hand, had six-year terms and answered not directly to the people but to the state legislatures. Presidents fell midway between the other two in length of term and were accountable to the people through the electoral college

---

[14] Ibid., No. 63, p. 384.
[15] Ibid., No. 71, p. 432.

mechanism. Those who charge that the indirect modes of election for senators and presidents screened them from public control overlook both the pronounced popular character of the early state legislatures and the extent to which the electoral college mechanism could (and did) function as a vehicle for the expression of popular sentiments. It is more accurate to interpret these devices as alternative ways of ensuring public accountability than as efforts to thwart accountability. The reason why they were chosen reveals an important aspect of the framers' plan for deliberation.

In the framers' view the distinct advantage of employing the state legislatures and the electoral college for selecting some political leaders was that these institutions could add to the expression of general popular preferences a degree of knowledge and deliberation usually lacking in direct popular elections. In a senatorial contest, for example, among several candidates all basically sympathetic to the interests and sentiments of the citizens of the state, the members of the state legislature would usually be more capable than the people themselves of choosing the one who would become the most effective national legislator—especially if the candidates were, or had been, state officials. Given the nature of the state legislatures in the founding period, it was extremely unlikely that senators would be chosen whose views were incompatible with the dominant dispositions of the state citizenry. (Even now the state legislature of Massachusetts, if it had the power, would be as unlikely to select as senator an individual with the views of a Strom Thurmond as would the legislature of South Carolina select someone with the views of an Edward Kennedy.) The framers made a similar argument about the benefits of having a select body of individuals, chosen for the purpose, actually elect the president. Even in this system, however, "the sense of the people" would operate, for the electors would themselves be selected either by the democratic state legislatures or by the people directly.[16] Under such a scheme the person chosen president would usually possess widespread popular support and share the general policy dispositions of the national community.

There was, then, good reason to think that those elected to the House, Senate, and presidency would bring with them into office a sensitivity to the interests and concerns of their constituents. If that sensitivity continued while they served, then the results of their deliberations would broadly approximate what the people themselves would have decided had they engaged in a similar reasoning process. That legislators and presidents will continue faithful to the deep-

---

[16] Ibid., No. 68, p. 412.

seated desires of their constituents is not guaranteed. Nonetheless, it is strongly encouraged by the reelection incentive, therefore by the personal interest of the office holder. Although the electoral connection is not perfect, it quite effectively discourages substantial deviations between the broad desires of constituents and the actions of representatives. To continue an earlier analogy, can it be seriously doubted that the voters of Massachusetts would refuse to reelect Senator Kennedy if over a period of several years he voted a straight conservative line in the Senate, or that the citizens of South Carolina would replace Strom Thurmond if he became a born-again liberal?

The Contribution of Bicameralism and Separation of Powers

While the framers designed their system of election and accountability to ensure a basic compatibility between the deliberations of representatives and the interests of the citizenry, they also understood that too much accountability could be dangerous to sound deliberation. If every national legislator served only a two-year term between elections, legislative deliberations would turn almost exclusively on short-range considerations, forcing from view the long-term consequences of national action. The six-year term for senators was designed in part to meet this problem. The purpose was not to undermine accountability but to make Congress more truly deliberative without sacrificing the popular connection. Ideally the Senate would pursue policies like those which would be desired by a responsible and far-sighted public. Viewed in this light, bicameralism was not a device to thwart majority rule but an institutional mechanism that would promote the effective rule of the deliberative majority.

Much the same can be said for the separation of powers between the Congress and presidency, one of the most distinctive features of American national government and one perennially criticized as antidemocratic. The president's veto power is particularly attacked as a device that may overrule majority sentiment expressed through Congress; for it seems to pit the personal views of one individual against considered community judgments expressed through two distinct representative bodies. A frequent use of the presidential veto to block legislative actions necessarily raises questions about the democratic character of the American political system.

In fact, presidents often claim that their veto actions conform more to majority opinion than the legislation they overturn. This claim is most plausible when the issue is one of partiality. Bicameralism may have nicely balanced short- and long-term considerations in the formulation of public policy, but it could not of itself have solved the problem of partiality. Each legislator represents only a portion of the whole; no one of them, whether in the House or Senate, can truly claim to speak for the entire nation. Even someone like Thomas Jefferson, who was not a public proponent of presidential power, maintained that it was especially the president who "command[ed] a view of the whole ground."[17] On some issues at least, a president may reasonably claim that his opinion more accurately represents majority sentiment than does the aggregation of views embodied in congressional actions, especially when a president articulates certain diffuse values which in any particular congressional district are less politically potent than other more tangible interests.[18]

One of the most extreme uses of the presidential veto raises the general issue clearly. In his first term as president (1885–1889), Grover Cleveland vetoed 413 laws duly passed by both branches of Congress. Of these only two were overridden. The numbers alone suggest that presidential action effectively undermined majority rule. Yet, the vast portion of these were vetoes of private bills, special laws to provide government pensions to specific Civil War veterans. Although Cleveland signed many such laws, others he viewed as grossly irresponsible, based upon dubious and unsubstantiated claims. In this exercise of the veto, Cleveland saw himself as upholding the broad public desire for economy in government against the narrow interests of legislators who sought to curry favor with local constituents.

The significance of the veto does not end with the addition of another voice claiming to speak the sentiments of the true national majority. The Constitution itself requires that the president publicly give his reasons whenever he vetoes a bill. His objections are laid before the House or Senate as reconsideration begins. The clear intention of this process was to raise the conflict above a battle of wills to a genuine contest of opinion and argument. Both the actual and threatened use of the veto will foster a kind of deliberation *between* the branches of government.

There is, finally, one other way in which the veto power fosters deliberation on public policy issues, but this was less the explicit intention of the framers than a natural working out of their system of government. Because he is forced to take stands on pending

---

[17] "First Inaugural" in *A Compilation of the Messages and Papers of the Presidents, 1789-1897*, ed. James D. Richardson, 10 vols. (Washington, D.C.: U.S. Government Printing Office, 1896-1899), vol. 1, p. 324.

[18] See, for example, the argument of Grant McConnell in *Private Power and American Democracy* (New York: Vintage Books, 1970), pp. 365-68 and passim.

national issues, the president is encouraged to become a public advocate of a certain course of national action. And it is a short step from advocating issues to informing and educating the people. The right kind of political instruction from our leaders can do much to promote informed and reasonable majorities.

The Responsiveness of Institutions

Having shown that the framers embraced an understanding of majority rule that was consistent with the need for certain kinds of restraints on majority desires and that their institutional mechanism was reasonably fashioned to achieve the effective rule of the deliberative majority, it remains to assess whether the system has actually worked as they intended. Simply asked, is there substantial evidence that throughout the course of American history deliberative majorities have been unable to work their will through the political branches of American national government? A precise answer to this question is impossible since, as has been argued, the deliberative sense of the community is created *through* the operation of the institutions; it does not usually exist outside the institutions in a way that can be measured and compared to governmental decisions. Nonetheless, there have been times in our history when a certain set of political ideas has predominated in the public mind, not as a short-lived or passing inclination but as a deep-seated and enduring public judgment about the purposes or goals of politics and the contribution of government to these ends.

In the early years of the Republic, the "revolution of 1800" infused into the national governing institutions the widely accepted principles of Jeffersonian republicanism. A generation later Jacksonian democracy gained ascendancy in the national councils. In the latter case the U.S. Senate—by design less responsive to shifts in public opinion than the House—engaged in a temporary holding action, going so far in 1834 as to condemn President Jackson formally for some of his controversial actions to dismantle the national bank, the cornerstone of Jackson's domestic policy. Within a few years, however, the growing democratic temper of the age had worked its way even through the Senate, rendering the upper chamber by 1837 a reliable partner of the president and House. The shift was the simple consequence of state legislators, devoted to the principles of Jacksonian democracy, electing as senators those of like persuasion. This kind of transformation takes longer for the Senate than the House, but not much longer.

The institutional success of these two social and political movements within the nation's first half-century is testimony to the remarkable openness of the framers' governmental design. If those who drafted our fundamental law in 1787 truly sought to establish a system that would protect and perpetuate the power and values of their particular social or economic class, they proved themselves unaccountably inept. That the responsiveness of the institutions to new ideas has continued well into the twentieth century is demonstrated by the success of the growing public liberalism of the 1930s, the so-called New Deal philosophy, in capturing the political institutions and guiding national policy for a generation.[19]

Deliberative Democracy and Other Interpretations

While the theory of deliberative democracy outlined here stands in sharpest contrast to "aristocratic" or "elitist" interpretations of the Constitution, it also differs in significant ways from other basically democratic interpretations. It may serve as a corrective to two broad tendencies present in these other interpretations.

One tendency is to depreciate the role of deliberation within the governing institutions by interpreting the framers' design as one in which the pursuit of personal interest by citizens and leaders alike will almost automatically work to foster the larger public good. At the level of the citizenry, the pursuit of material well-being in a large commercial society will deflect attention from historically divisive distinctions of religion or economic class, while simultaneously rendering unjust majorities less able to work their will. At the governmental level, the separation of powers and checks and balances will pit ambition against ambition and thereby guard against tyranny from the top.[20]

Although the multiplicity of interests may solve the problem of majority faction, and institutional design may meet the danger of usurpation, neither will ensure that the positive business of governing will be done well. Sound public policy demands more than the pursuit of private ambition. It requires also leaders of knowledge and experi-

---

[19] For an excellent discussion of this point, see Samuel H. Beer, "In Search of a New Public Philosophy" in Anthony King, ed., *The New American Political System* (Washington, D.C.: American Enterprise Institute, 1978), pp. 5-44.

[20] For this interpretation of the framers' plan, see generally the works of Martin Diamond, especially "Democracy and *The Federalist*: A Reconsideration of the Framers' Intent," *American Political Science Review*, vol. 53 (March 1959), pp. 52-68 and "The Federalist" in Leo Strauss and Joseph Cropsey, ed., *History of Political Philosophy*, 2d ed. (Chicago: Rand McNally, 1972), pp. 631-51.

ence who work in a setting that fosters collective deliberation about "the permanent and aggregate interests of the community."[21] This has been largely overlooked by the contemporary pluralist school, which, while finding the system basically democratic, attributes the outcomes of policy disputes to little more than logrolling and compromise among special interest advocates.

The other tendency among those who argue the essential democratic nature of the Constitution is to reduce the democratic principle to little more than the people's right to select their leaders. Theorists like Willmoore Kendall accord great importance to deliberation by wise and virtuous representatives, but the connection between that deliberation and community wishes seems tenuous at best.[22] Although Kendall presumes that governmental decisions will reflect the "deliberate sense of the community," it is not clear why, since for Kendall the function of elections is simply to identify the "virtuous men," not to argue and debate policy issues. Indeed, in Kendall's view, the constitutional system rests "on the ability of the people, i.e., at least a majority of the people, to make sound judgments regarding the virtues of their neighbors, not on the ability of the people to deliberate on matters of policy."[23]

The problem with applying this essentially Burkean view of representation to the American system is that it vastly underestimates the role which policy issues would necessarily play in campaigns for national office. Why would—or should—citizens restrict their considerations to the identification of the virtuous when, in any diverse and dynamic political community, the virtuous themselves will disagree about many of the most important matters facing the nation? In this, the virtuous mirror the diversity of interests and opinions among the public generally.

Not only is some degree of policy discussion likely in an election campaign, but it is also necessary in order to ensure that those selected to positions of authority will share the basic interests, dispositions, and attitudes of the citizenry. As long as candidates are not forced to commit themselves to specific policy proposals—especially nonincumbents who have yet to study the salient issues in a legislative setting—and as long as representatives are not recallable between elections—which would subject them to control by unreflective public opinion

---

[21] *Federalist* No. 10, p. 78.

[22] See especially his "The Two Majorities" in, among other collections, Ronald C. Moe, ed., *Congress and the President* (Pacific Palisades, Calif.: Goodyear Publishing Company, 1971), pp. 270-89.

[23] Ibid., p. 285.

—then policy discussion throughout a campaign will not foreclose subsequent deliberation on the details of legislative policy. While the framers put great faith in the principle of representation, it would be a mistake to overstate the intended independence of representatives from majority sentiment in the system they designed. The electoral process is the key.[24]

Threats to the Deliberative Majority

Although the Constitution was designed to make the deliberative majority the effective ruling power in the United States, we cannot simply assume that it continues to achieve this end. The framers' document is now nearly two hundred years old. Since its drafting, the American political system has undergone enormous change, through reinterpretation of constitutional provisions, formal amendment to the Constitution, and such extraconstitutional developments as the rise (and fall?) of political parties, as well as general economic and social change. From what directions, then, are likely to come the most serious threats to the rule of the deliberative majority in contemporary America?

Perhaps the most common version of the charge that the American political system is currently undemocratic is that the moneyed few, especially corporate and business interests, have subverted the forms of democracy for their own narrow ends. This view is embraced by many who criticize the original Constitution as elitist: "Public policies, whether formulated by conservatives or liberals, Republicans or Democrats, fairly consistently favor the large corporate interests at a substantial cost to many millions of workers, small farmers, small producers, consumers, taxpayers, low-income people, urban slum dwellers, indigent elderly and rural poor."[25] Corporate power dominates formal democracy because either (1) the crucial decisions are made outside the political system, that is, in the boardrooms; (2) the wealthy interests have "captured" the institutions of government; or (3) these same interests have manipulated public opinion. It sometimes seems as if the frequency and intensity of such critiques of the American political system vary proportionately with the growth of government programs directed to the very groups who occupy the lowest rungs of the American economic ladder. In any case, this version of

---

[24] A contrary position is taken by Walter Berns in his essay in this volume. Berns maintains that in the framers' view "the persons elected to public office should not reflect the people who choose them. . . ." The people "elect representatives but the persons they elect do not represent them!"

[25] Parenti, *Democracy for the Few*, p. 316.

the undemocratic charge should not deflect our attention from other threats to the rule of the deliberative majority.

In recent years a growing number of students of the American political scene have noted that the issue of "elite" control of political decisions is not restricted to economic distinctions. There is mounting evidence that those who participate most intensely in politics are significantly more liberal or conservative than the rank-and-file of the two major political parties. This raises the possibility that political decisions will be skewed in one direction or the other, depending on the party in power. The electoral connection will moderate this tendency somewhat, but less and less as nonelected officials drawn from the pool of political activists gain ever greater influence in American government—whether congressional or presidential staff, bureaucrats, federal judges, or members of those "issue networks" which are now an integral part of the Washington community. If a scheme of public accountability is essential to ensure that "the cool and deliberate sense of the community . . . will . . . ultimately prevail over the views of its rulers," then we may well wonder whether recent trends threaten to replace the rule of the deliberative majority with the more "enlightened" views of the left or right.

In the end, however, the greatest threat may come from an entirely different direction, namely from the modern movement for the direct democracy rejected by the framers. The recent proposal for a constitutional amendment that would allow the people to make their own laws through a process of initiative and referendum is a prominent manifestation of the desire to free the people from dependence on their elected representatives. By circumventing representation, however, this proposal jeopardizes the deliberation that representation fosters. No doubt a kind of communitywide deliberation would accompany any referendum contest, but such popular consideration is likely to be influenced profoundly by slick advertising campaigns, the most immoderate voices on each side of the controversy, and the passions of the moment. To repeat an earlier point, sound deliberation requires both extensive knowledge and a setting which promotes collective reasoning about common goals. Although Congress is far from the perfect deliberative institution, it more closely approximates the requirements for sound deliberation than could be expected in most any legislative contest conducted in an assembly of two hundred million.

Finally, this proposal reminds us that the principle of deliberation is, as it were, built into the governmental system by the original written Constitution. After all, the proposal takes the form of an *amend-*

ment to the Constitution. Without that amendment elected representatives will retain the minimum degree of discretion and independent judgment necessary to withstand the demands of unreflective popular sentiments and thereby foster the rule of a reasonable and informed public. The Constitution, it appears, is not merely what the Supreme Court says it is, what historians, political scientists, or law professors say it is, or even what each generation of Americans says it is. It is also a set of political institutions that embody in their structure and functioning enduring principles of sound popular government.

7

Conservatives, the Constitution, and the "Spirit of Accommodation"

Alfred F. Young

On June 18, 1787, a very hot Monday in Philadelphia, Alexander Hamilton delivered a five- to six-hour address at the Constitutional Convention, easily the longest and very likely the most curious speech made to the convention. From the premise that "all communities divide themselves . . . into the rich and the well-born," adding the corollary that "the mass of people . . . seldom judge or determine right," the delegate from New York moved to his ideal for an American government. He proposed a president and senate elected for life ("to serve during good behavior") and a house popularly elected for a three-year term. The president would have an absolute "negative" over the congress and the power to appoint the governors of each state, who in turn could veto any state law. If others quickly saw a resemblance to a king, House of Lords, and House of Commons, they were not mistaken; the British constitution, in Hamilton's opinion, was "the best model the world has ever produced."[1]

As important as the speech was, so too was the delegates' reaction. There was no discussion; the session adjourned. Gouverneur Morris called the speech "the most able and impressive he had ever heard." Three days later, William Samuel Johnson was more or less accurate in saying that Hamilton's proposals "had been praised by everybody [but] he has been supported by none." A few days later, Hamilton absented himself for a month. He was not exactly a pariah;

NOTE: The author expresses appreciation to Morton J. Frisch and Jackson T. Main for suggestions they made in response to a draft of this paper and to Robert Goldwin and William Schambra for patient editorial assistance.

[1] "Constitutional Convention Speech on a Plan of Government," Harold Syrett, ed., *The Papers of Alexander Hamilton* (New York: Columbia University Press, 1962), vol. 4, pp. 178-207 (in particular, pp. 192, 200); "Plan for Government," pp. 207-211.

George Washington pleaded with him to return. He did, to play a part in the final deliberations and then sign the finished document claiming "no plan was more remote from his own."[2]

The paths not taken in history often shed light on the paths taken. Douglass Adair has argued with his usual cogency that "we mistake the significance of Hamilton's proposal of an elective monarch as a solution of the crisis of 1787 if we think of his plan as either *original* or *unrepresentative* of the thought of important segments of American opinion in 1787."[3] To understand not so much why Hamilton brought forth his plan but why the convention rejected it, is an avenue into the heart of the Constitution.

In this essay I will argue that the Constitution was the work of accommodating conservatives who drafted an essentially middle-of-the-road document that, by its very nature, produced different responses among contemporaries of a democratic bent. To develop this argument, we will need to explore the political experiences of the revolutionary generation. We will turn, first, to the democratic movement and thought that emerged with popular mass resistance to Britain after 1765 and, second, to the variant conservative responses to this threat. We will then return to the Constitutional Convention to probe the way conservatives were impelled in democratic directions. Finally, we will examine the responses to the Constitution in the controversy over ratification of men who might be considered democratic: those who were hostile, those who gave it qualified support, and those who gave it an enthusiastic endorsement. Taken together, this exploration may contribute toward answering the question, How democratic is the Constitution? by answering the question, How democratic was it in 1787?

The Democratic Threat

By the spring of 1774, the democratic threat once implicit in mass participation in the resistance to Great Britain was explicit. No one caught this more vividly than Gouverneur Morris, a twenty-three-year-old scion of the owner of Morrisania, a large tenanted estate in Westchester County, as he observed a huge mass meeting in New York City:

---

[2] Broadus Mitchell, *Alexander Hamilton* (New York: Macmillan, 1957), vol. 1, pp. 391-392.

[3] Douglass Adair, "Experience Must be Our Only Guide: History, Democratic Theory, and the United States Constitution," in Trevor Colbourn, ed., *Fame and the Founding Fathers: Essays by Douglass Adair* (New York: Norton, 1974), p. 117.

I stood on the balcony and on my right hand were ranged all the people of property, with some few poor dependents, and on the other the tradesmen, etc., who thought it worth their while to leave daily labour for the good of the country. . . . The mob begin to think and reason. Poor reptiles! it is with them a vernal morning; they are struggling to cast off their winter's slough, they bask in the sunshine, and ere noon they will bite, depend upon it. The gentry begin to fear this. . . . I see, and I see it with fear and trembling, that if the disputes with *Great Britain* continue, we shall be under the worst of all possible dominions; we shall be under the domination of a riotous mob.

More than tactics was at stake: "They fairly contended about the future forms of our Government, whether it should be founded upon aristocratic or democratic principles." [4]

What Morris captured was a moment in a process. A popular movement that had begun with "mob" actions in 1765 was transforming itself. Sons of Liberty organizations led by lawyers, sea captains, lesser merchants, and prosperous artisans were giving way to self-led Committees of Mechanics (the term for skilled craftsmen); crowd actions were giving way to public meetings; formerly deferential mechanics were insisting on direct representation on committees. By the spring of 1776, with independence a prospect and a state constitution to be drafted in New York City, a Committee of Mechanics insisted it was "a right which God has given them in common with all men, to judge whether it be consistent with their interest to accept or reject a constitution." The process was to continue with the transfer of power into the hands of endless committees: committees to enforce boycotts, committees to represent the militia, committees of safety, committees to detect conspiracies. [5]

---

[4] G. Morris to John Penn, May 20, 1774, in U.S. Congress, *American Archives*, Peter Force, comp., Washington, D.C., 1837-1853, vol. 1, pp. 342-343. For recent scholarship on popular movements, see Alfred F. Young, ed., *The American Revolution: Explorations in the History of American Radicalism* (DeKalb: Northern Illinois University Press, 1976); for the reflections of two leading scholars of the subject, see Merrill Jensen, "The American Revolution and the American People," *Journal of American History*, vol. 57 (1970), pp. 3-35 and *The Revolution Within America* (New York: New York University Press, 1974), and Richard B. Morris, " 'We the People of the United States': The Bicentennial of a People's Revolution," *American Historical Review*, vol. 82 (1977), pp. 1-19.

[5] "The Respectful Address of the Mechanics in Union," *New York Gazette*, June 17, 1776; Richard Ryerson, *The Revolution is Now Begun: The Radical Committees of Philadelphia, 1765-1776* (Philadelphia: University of Pennsylvania Press, 1978); Edward Countryman, "Consolidating Power in Revolutionary America: The Case of New York, 1775-1783," *Journal of Interdisciplinary History*, vol. 6 (1976), pp. 545-678.

In 1776, Thomas Paine's *Common Sense* registered still another moment in the process: the flowering of a democratic ideology. It is difficult not to exaggerate the importance of the pamphlet that went through twenty-five editions in 1776 alone and was probably read by several hundred thousand people (and read to thousands more), at a time when a newspaper might reach 2,000, or a pamphlet perhaps 5,000. It is crucial to recall that Paine offered much more than an argument for independence. He began with a section, "Of the origin and design of government in general," and moved to "Of monarchy and hereditary succession" before he reached "Thoughts on the present state of American Affairs" and concluded with further thoughts on a "Continental Charter."[6]

Paine rejected not only King George III but also monarchy in principle, not only British policies but also "the so much boasted Constitution of England," attacking the underlying assumptions of hierarchy, hereditary rulers, and mixed or balanced government. The pamphlet precipitated not only a debate with Tories over independence but with conservative advocates of independence. John Adams, for example, who thought *Common Sense* "so democratical, without any restraint or even an attempt at equilibrium or Counterpoise, that it must produce confusion and every Evil work," rushed into print with *Thoughts on Government* to tutor America's novice constitution makers.[7]

Paine's creed—it was a set of "hints," he said, not a systematic political science—stressed simple government: "The more simple a thing is, the less liable it is to be disordered, and the easier repaired when disordered." Direct democracy was the ideal, but, that being impossible, elected representatives should mirror their constituents and be elected from convenient districts, at frequent intervals, "because . . . the *elected* might by that means return and mix again with the general body of the electors in a few months." "Let the [state] assemblies be annual, with a President only. The representation more equal," ran an afterthought.[8]

In his vision of a "continental" government, Paine's central principle was "a large and equal representation." A congress should be elected directly by the voters, with the states divided into districts,

---

[6] Philip Foner, ed., *The Complete Works of Thomas Paine* (New York: Citadel Press, 1945), vol. 1, pp. 3-46; Eric Foner, *Tom Paine and Revolutionary America* (New York: Oxford University Press, 1976), pp. 81 ff., 120 ff.

[7] John Adams, "Thoughts on Government," in Charles F. Adams, ed., *The Works of John Adams* (Boston: Little, Brown, 1854), vol. 4, pp. 193-200.

[8] Paine, *Common Sense*, pp. 5-6.

each sending "at least thirty" representatives, for a total of at least 390. A president would be elected by the congress on a rotating basis, from among the states, with decisions made by a three-fifths majority. He also proposed a separate body, "a Continental Conference," to draft a "Continental Charter answering to what is called the Magna Charta of England." This conference would be chosen indirectly by a combination of congressmen, state assemblymen, and "representatives of the people at large" assembled "from all parts of the province for that purpose." And it would secure "freedom and property to all men and above all things the free exercise of religion . . . with such other matters as is necessary for a charter to contain."[9]

These hints guided a great many men as they confronted the task of erecting constitutions in their independent states in 1776 and, it is not too much to claim, as they confronted the federal Constitution in 1787–1788. Paine said relatively little about structures, however.

The Pennsylvania constitution, a victory of radical democrats, may be taken as the democratic creed fulfilled at its extreme. A Declaration of Rights preceded it. The structure was simple: a one-house legislature with a weak, plural executive. Representation was from districts newly apportioned by population (to be reapportioned at seven-year intervals). Elections were annual and rotation required; no one could serve more than four years in seven. There were no property qualifications for any office (only an oath of allegiance to the new state). Suffrage was open to all taxpayers. Popular participation in the legislative process was the goal: The assembly was to be open; the votes and proceedings were to be published. More important, a bill could not become a law until, after the first reading, it was publicized throughout the colony, discussed, and voted upon at the following session. The executive was to carry out the will of the assembly (it was a twelve-person council, elected for three-year terms, with one-third rotating every year). A Council of Censors, popularly elected, was to review the constitutionality of laws at seven-year intervals. Supreme Court judges were to be appointed by the executive council for seven-year terms, subject to removal by the assembly for misbehavior. Other court officials, for example, justices of the peace and sheriffs, were to be selected by the council from candidates elected by popular vote each year. Finally, under the Pennsylvania constitution, even militia officers were to be popularly elected.[10]

---

9 Ibid., pp. 27-29.

10 *The Federal and State Constitutions, and Other Organic Laws*, ed. Francis N. Thorpe, 7 vols. (Washington, D.C.: U.S. Government Printing Office, 1909), vol. 7, pp. 3815-3819.

In only one important respect did the Pennsylvania constitution fall short of a widely held democratic ideal. Its architects introduced, but later withdrew, what contemporaries called an "agrarian" clause:

> That [since] an enormous proportion of property vested in a few individuals is dangerous to the rights, and destructive of the common happiness of mankind ... therefore every free state hath a right by its laws to discourage the possession of such property.[11]

One should be wary, however, of making the Pennsylvania constitution the exclusive litmus test for democratic political thought. Relatively few democrats seem to have argued for a unicameral legislature (only Pennsylvania, Vermont, and Georgia adopted it). As for suffrage, a good many democrats were wary of venturing beyond a small-freehold property qualification, especially where there were large dependent populations like the Hudson Valley tenants. More important, it was a time when ideas were in flux. Many ordinary men awakening to political consciousness had to find their own minds. As John Jay said of the committee drafting New York's constitution, "Our politicians are like some guests at a feast, are perplexed and undetermined which dish to prefer." We need also to remind ourselves that there was a war on and a need to preserve a coalition.[12]

The war intensified the democratizing process. David Ramsay, the South Carolina physician who in 1789 wrote one of the first histories of the Revolution, caught this moment in the process:

> When the war began, the Americans were a mass of husbandmen, merchants, mechanics and fishermen, but the necessities of the country gave a spring to the active powers of the inhabitants and set them on thinking, speaking and acting in a line far beyond that to which they had been accustomed. ... It seemed as if the war not only required but created talents.[13]

---

[11] Pennsylvania Archives, 3rd ser., vol. 10, p. 762, cited in Foner, ed., Tom Paine, p. 44.

[12] Cited in Alfred F. Young, The Democratic Republicans of New York: The Origins, 1763-1797 (Chapel Hill: University of North Carolina Press, 1967), p. 18; for the state constitutions in comparative perspective, see Jackson Turner Main, The Sovereign States, 1775-1783 (New York: Franklin Watts, 1973), and Elisha Douglass, Rebels and Democrats: The Struggle for Equal Political Rights and Majority Rule During the American Revolution (Chapel Hill: University of North Carolina Press, 1955), and Robert R. Palmer, The Age of the Democratic Revolution (Princeton, N.J.: Princeton University Press, 1959), vol. 1, pp. 217-238.

[13] David Ramsay, The History of the American Revolution (Philadelphia: R. Aitken & Son, 1789), vol. 1, pp. 315-316.

One consequence, particularly after the war, was an increase in participation in the political process: more people voting, more seeking public office. Mechanics, for example, who formerly endorsed one of their betters, now sought office; the ad hoc Committee of Mechanics became a permanent General Society of Mechanics and Tradesmen.[14]

As a major result of all this ferment, the social composition of the state legislatures shifted downward a notch, and sometimes more. Contemporaries spoke of the "new men," "the raw new hands," and the "better sort" sniffed at "men unimproved by education and unrefined by honor" who now framed laws. The New York legislature, dominated before the war by Livingstons, Schuylers, Van Rensselaers, Delanceys, and Beekmans, "gentlemen" all, did not try, after the war, to raise a quorum at harvest time; too many members were plain farmers.[15] Jackson Turner Main, the scholar who has given the subject the most assiduous attention, has provided elaborate quantitative proof of this shift. What is striking is that it occurred in the senates, designed to be the protectors of large property, as well as in assemblies.[16] This point, at which the democratic movement of the revolutionary era had perhaps its greatest impact, the state legislatures, had the most threatening potential to conservatives.

Conservative Responses

The democratic political movement was a pervasive force in the revolutionary era, helping to shape the response of every major political group: popular patriot leaders, loyalists, and conservative patriots. The "mob" was a problem to popular leaders no less than to Gouverneur Morris. The recent scholarship of Pauline Maier has made clear that, for over a decade, Sons of Liberty leaders like Samuel Adams were waging a war on two fronts: to pressure Britain and to control the movements from below. "No violence or you'll hurt the cause," literally was their slogan in Boston. In 1775, Adams was informed by his ally, Elbridge Gerry, a merchant, that a government

---

[14] Staughton Lynd, "The Mechanics in New York Politics, 1774-1778," *Labor History*, vol. 5 (1964), pp. 215-246; Alfred F. Young, "The Mechanics and the Jeffersonians: New York, 1789-1801," ibid., pp. 247-276; for the general process, Gordon Wood, "The Democratization of Mind in the American Revolution," in U.S. Library of Congress, *Leadership in the American Revolution*, Washington, D.C., 1974, pp. 63-88.

[15] Young, *Democratic Republicans*, p. 27.

[16] Jackson Turner Main, *The Upper House in Revolutionary America, 1763-1788* (Madison: University of Wisconsin Press, 1967) and "Government by the People: The American Revolution and the Democratization of the Legislature," *William and Mary Quarterly*, 3rd ser., vol. 22 (1966), pp. 319-407.

had to be established as quickly as possible to replace the British because "the people are fully possessed of their dignity from the frequent delineation of their rights. . . . They now feel rather too much their own importance, and it requires great skill to produce such subordination as is necessary." Adams agreed. Men like Adams and Patrick Henry were not "radicals," if that term is defined as favoring internal political democracy; both followed John Adams's lead on balanced constitutions and a due "subordination." They were radical only toward Britain. They might have agreed "vox populi, vox dei," but they retained their following (which included men in their "establishments" as well as among the commonality) on the basis of their effective, militant leadership in the cause against Britain.[17]

Loyalist men of wealth, it might be argued, were victims of the mob. Many became loyalists in good part from the Gouverneur Morris syndrome, from a fear of their total inability to cope with the mob, especially when transformed into a democratic movement. A number of misleading stereotypes about loyalists have been corrected in recent years. Not all rich men became Tories; on the contrary the dominant wealth of Massachusetts, including Boston, and Virginia, the two centers of the Revolution, was patriot. Not all Tories were rich men; a strain of loyalism and "disaffection" existed among poor white farmers and black slaves who, with a kind of inverted class feeling, took the opposite stand from their patriot masters or landlords. A large number of the rich, however, especially in the middle colonies, were loyalist. Aristocratic, ridden with the prejudices of their class toward the "meaner sort," unequipped to take part in the hurly-burly of politics, they lacked any models for coping with a popular movement save that of repression or coercion. Accordingly, they abdicated political responsibility (as in Philadelphia), became political and military collaborators with the British (as in New York), or went into exile (as did 100,000 during and after the war).[18]

Conservative patriots were drawn from the same social sources as loyalists: merchant elites of the cities, landlord estate holders of the Hudson Valley, prosperous slaveholders in the South. Why some men raised with a certain set of conservative social values should turn Tory and others Whig, remains a mystery and a matter of general

---

[17] Pauline Maier, *From Resistance to Revolution: Colonial Radicals and the Development of American Opposition to Britain, 1765-1776* (New York: Knopf, 1972) and "Coming to Terms with Sam Adams," *American Historical Review,* vol. 81 (1976), pp. 12-37; Elbridge Gerry cited in Jensen, "The American People and the American Revolution," p. 31; Dirk Hoerder, *Crowd Action in Revolutionary Massachusetts, 1765-1780* (New York: Academic Press, 1977).

[18] Main, *Sovereign States,* chap. 8.

interest, because the split seems to recur in America's history. The experience of the revolutionary era suggests it may have something to do with the degree of confidence men of wealth had in their ability to deal with democratic movements.

The New York elite offers a case study. Gouverneur Morris's metaphor for the mob was a reptile that might bite; one had to scotch a snake, it was impossible to tame it. He also referred to the mob as a horse that had to be whipped. Robert R. Livingston, his associate, had a metaphor more apropos for the tactic he and his fellow conservatives adopted. He was convinced of "the propriety of Swimming with a Stream which it is impossible to stem." On the completion of New York's constitution in 1777, he contrasted the success of his friends with the failure of their counterparts in Pennsylvania: "I long ago advised that they should yield to the torrent if they hoped to direct its course—you know nothing but welltimed delays, indefatigable circumstance could have prevented our being exactly in their situation."[19]

The New Yorkers had begun years before—Livingston, John Jay, James Duane, Philip Schuyler, foremost among them—teaching themselves the tactic of "swimming with the stream" in committee sessions, in electoral politics, and at public meetings. Their task was formidable, facing as they did rivals in the Sons of Liberty and politically conscious mechanics, a merchant landlord elite that was probably more than half Tory, their own tenantry ready to take to arms, and yeomanry who would have nothing to do with "great men."

The New York constitution of 1777 was their handiwork. The provisions for voting typify the compromise written into the entire document. Governor and senators would be elected by voters with 100 pound freeholds; members of the assembly by voters with 20 pound freeholds or men who paid forty shillings rent. The governor would be elected by written ballot, the other officials by voice voting (which might be discontinued after the war). The governor, elected for a three-year term, would have veto power over legislation exercised jointly with a Council of Revision composed of the high judges, and appointive power exercised with the Council of Appointment, composed of four senators. The concessions to democracy were annual assembly elections, a written ballot, larger representation, and compulsory reapportionment. Had extreme conserva-

---

[19] Robert R. Livingston to William Duer, June 12, 1777, R. R. Livingston Papers, New York Historical Society; Staughton Lynd, "A Governing Class on the Defensive: The Case of New York" in *Class Conflict, Slavery, and the United States Constitution* (Indianapolis: Bobbs-Merrill, 1967).

tives prevailed, there would have been elections at four-year intervals by voice voting and an upper house and governor chosen indirectly. Had the democrats won, there might have been taxpayer suffrage, a written ballot in all elections, annual election for all offices, and no executive veto. A contemporary said of the result that it "preserved a proper line between Aristocracy on the one hand and Democracy on the other." It was so delicately balanced, said John Jay, that "another turn of the winch would have cracked the cord."[20]

The machinery, however, did not work quite as intended. In the first election, Philip Schuyler was defeated for governor by George Clinton, whose "family and connections," said Schuyler, "do not entitle him to so distinguished a predominance." The conservatives, having lost, then formed a coalition with Clinton. He appointed them to high positions and he quelled the tenant rebellion that threatened their estates. They supported him politically until the mid-1780s. On the other hand, they could neither control nor influence the "new men" in the New York state legislature. Once this was clear, they turned to national power to curb the state power that had eluded them. Then they broke with Clinton. Years later, after Livingston broke with the Federalists to rejoin Clinton, he spoke of returning to a "close union of the Livingston family with the democratic interests of the state."[21]

The New York experience of 1777—so rich in implications for 1787—may have been more typical than historians have allowed. As Jackson Main writes, after subjecting the state constitutions to exhaustive scrutiny, "Whig thought seldom appeared in pure form, and when put into practice the pull of democratic ideology distorted the blessed symmetry of a balanced government. In the same fashion, adherents of democracy, confronting both practical circumstances and a determined opposition, diluted their ideal with Whig accretions." In most states, the two ideologies "compromised and the resultant moderate constitutions reflected therefore a kind of consensus, genuinely accepted by many Americans, incorporating ideas shared by Whigs and democrats alike."[22]

---

[20] Robert Troup to John Jay, May 15, 1777, in Richard Morris, ed., *John Jay, The Making of a Revolutionary: Unpublished Papers, 1745-1780* (New York: Harper & Row, 1975), p. 403, and p. 394 for Jay's comment; for the New York constitution, Bernard Mason, *The Road to Independence: The Revolutionary Movement in New York, 1773-1777* (Lexington: University of Kentucky Press, 1966).

[21] Young, *Democratic Republicans*, chap. 1-3; Schuyler cited at p. 2, Livingston at p. 291.

[22] Main, *Sovereign States*, pp. 144, 185.

The gentry in Maryland offer a different case study: They consolidated their power by an ultraconservative constitution first, then they appeased the underclasses to maintain their authority. In Maryland, in addition to a large class of poor whites, tenants, and freeholders, slaves composed 25 percent of the population (40 to 50 percent in some areas). Ten percent of the whites controlled 50 percent of the wealth, 20 percent controlled 75 percent of the wealth.[23]

Charles Carroll of Carrollton enables us to follow the attitudes of this elite. Enthusiastic in 1773 for resistance to Britain, by 1776 he was fearful the colonies "would be ruined" by the "bad governments" that would be "simple democracies." He joined his fellow men of large property to draft a constitution in which property alone ruled. To be a member of the lower house, a man had to own a minimum of 500 pounds' worth of real or personal property; to be a member of the upper house or the governor's council, or sheriff, a minimum of 1,000 pounds'; and to be governor, 5,000 pounds' or more. Voters elected only members of the lower house, the sheriffs and members of an electoral college; the electors would select the senators, who, in turn (with the members of the house), would select the governor. Under these provisions, only 10.9 percent of all adult white males in Maryland were qualified to serve in the house and only 7.4 percent in the senate.[24]

The consolidation of elite control only worsened the enormous disaffection from the patriot cause within Maryland, leading to outright loyalist resistance, refusal to do military service, insubordination in the militia, unrest among the slaves, and the threat of poor-white support for slave insurrection. The elite was patriot, and, as the most recent scholar of Maryland politics has explained, in 1777 they "anxiously sought to save both their class and the Revolution by popularizing the movement for independence." Their solution, writes Roland Hoffman, was a fiscal program "aimed at subduing the class antagonisms that underlay much of the internal protest": a tax system under which the planter elite assumed a greater burden and a tender law that in effect "voided the bulk of all internal credit obligations," severely affecting them as creditors.[25]

Charles Carroll of Annapolis, father of the Carrollton Carroll, and a large moneylender, was enraged; if the lawmakers went so far,

---

23 Ronald Hoffman, "The 'Disaffected' in the Revolutionary South," in Young, ed., *American Revolution*, p. 280.

24 Ronald Hoffman, "Popularizing the Revolution: Internal Conflict and Economic Sacrifice in Maryland, 1774-1780," *Maryland Historical Magazine* (1974), pp. 129-130.

25 Cited in Hoffman, "The Disaffected," pp. 306-307.

what was to stop them from saying, "No man shall hold above 500 acres of land"? His son explained the need of conciliation: "The law suits the multitudes, individuals must submit to partial losses; no great revolutions can happen in a state without revolutions or mutations of private property." He was candid: "I have long considered our personal estate, I mean the monied part of it, to be in jeopardy," he explained. "If we can save a third of that and all our lands and Negroes I shall think ourselves well off." "There is a time when it is wisdom to yield to injustice and to popular heresies and delusions." The alternative was worse: "violence and greater injustice."[26]

Thus, in variant ways, the gentry in New York and Maryland weathered the storm of the Revolution. From the mid-1780s on, it could be argued that the gentry, north and south, faced another storm, if not in their own states, in their neighbors'. There was a general crisis in the "system"—a word in common usage—a new threat that was difficult to accommodate.

Scholars traditionally have emphasized Shays' Rebellion in Massachusetts in 1786 as a catalyst to conservatives. They are not wrong. There were "combustibles in every State, which a spark might set fire to," as Washington stated and as recent scholarship has verified.[27] One of James Madison's principal complaints in 1787 was the "want of guaranty to the states of their constitutions and laws against internal violence." But there was, in a sense, a danger worse than rebellion. The defeated Shaysites were turning to state elections, said Madison, "by endeavoring to give the elections such a turn as may promote their views under the auspices of Constitutional forms." What, he asked, if they succeeded? This then would be legal Shaysism: a danger for which there seemingly was no remedy.[28]

In state after state, the "new men" were able to pass, or threatened to pass, paper currency laws, mortgage stay laws, and tax laws shifting burdens to the rich. As Madison stated,

> Debtors have defrauded their creditors. The landed interest has borne hard on the mercantile interest. The Holders of one species of property have thrown a disproportion of taxes on the holders of another species.

---

[26] Ibid.

[27] Washington to Henry Knox, December 26, 1786, *The Writings of George Washington*, ed. John C. Fitzpatrick, 39 vols. (Washington, D.C.: U.S. Government Printing Office, 1931-1949); Robert Becker, " 'Combustibles in Every State': A Frame of Reference for Shays' Rebellion" (forthcoming), developed in part in Becker, *Revolution, Reform and the Policies of American Taxation, 1763-1783* (Baton Rouge: University of Louisiana Press, 1980).

[28] Madison to Jefferson, April 23, 1787, in Julian Boyd, ed., *The Jefferson Papers* (Princeton, N.J.: Princeton University Press, 1958), vol. 11, p. 307.

These were the "Vices of the Political System of the United States" Madison had in mind on the eve of the Constitutional Convention in 1787, in the memorandum to himself that became the basis of several speeches at the convention and later of the equally important *Federalist* No. 10.[29]

The vices of the state governments as a major factor impelling conservatives to stronger national government is a theme that has found its historian in Gordon Wood. As Madison summarized it for Jefferson in 1787, these vices "contributed more to that uneasiness which produced the Convention and prepared the public mind for a general reform, than those which accrued to our national character and interest from the inadequacy of the Confederation to its immediate objectives."[30] Hamilton, in his private "conjectures," said the same thing; he counted among the "circumstances" in favor of the Constitution "the good will of most men of property in the several states who wish a government of the union able to protect them against domestic violence and the depredations which the democratic spirit is apt to make on property."[31]

As Madison reflected on these vices in the state governments, he was impelled to generalize about their causes, an analysis he made famous in *Federalist* No. 10.

> All civilized societies are divided into different interests and factions, as they happen to be creditors or debtors—rich or poor—husbandmen, merchants or manufacturers—members of different religious sects—followers of different political leaders—inhabitants of different districts—owners of different kinds of property &c &c

The problem was that

> in republican government the majority however composed, ultimately give the law. Whenever therefore an apparent or common passion unites a majority what is to restrain them

[29] Madison, "Vices of the Political System," April 1787, in William T. Hutchinson et al., eds., *The Papers of James Madison* (Chicago: University of Chicago Press, 1962), vol. 9, pp. 345-358; for convention versions, see Max Farrand, ed., *The Records of the Federal Convention of 1787* (New Haven: Yale University Press, 1937), vol. 1, pp. 135-336, 421-423. The quotation is from the convention version, p. 136.

[30] Madison to Jefferson, October 24, 1787, *Papers of Madison*, vol. 1, pp. 205-220; Gordon Wood, *The Creation of the American Republic, 1776-1787* (Chapel Hill: University of North Carolina Press, 1969), especially chap. 9, part 4.

[31] Hamilton, "Conjectures About the New Constitution," probably September 17-30, in Syrett, ed., *Papers of Hamilton*, vol. 4, pp. 275-276.

from unjust violations of the rights and interests of the minority, or of individuals? [32]

The notion "honesty is the best policy," "a respect for character," and "religion" were inadequate. One solution lay in "an enlargement of the sphere" of government.

> not because the impulse of a common interest or passion is less predominant in this case with the majority; but because a common interest or passion is less apt to be felt and the requisite combinations less easy to be formed by a great than a small number. The Society becomes broken into a greater variety of interests, of pursuits of passions, which check each other, whilst those who may feel a common sentiment have less opportunity of communication and concert.

An "extensive republic" was therefore one remedy to the "vices" of "a small republic." A second remedy, which Madison developed elsewhere, was a national "negative" or veto of state legislation. [33]

Thus, as conservatives became Founding Fathers, their priority was to counter the powers of the states with national power. On this score, they were not in any "spirit of accommodation." To achieve this priority, however, they were ready to practice the accommodation they had mastered in the decade and more gone by.

The Constitutional Convention and Accommodation

At the Philadelphia Convention in 1787, the chief architects of the Constitution were conservatives, either of an accommodating cast of mind (like Madison and James Wilson) or of an "ultra" cast of mind (like Gouverneur Morris). The delegates, if analyzed according to their experience with the political conflicts we have been describing, either (1) had direct experience within their own states with the threat of democratic movements, (2) like James Madison, were attuned to these threats by virtue of their position as national leaders in the Congress; or (3) were tutored at the convention by those who had such experiences. If they were not accommodating—and many were not—they nonetheless took part in a process of accommodation in which a middle-of-the-road constitution was the end-product.

The delegations from the three states we have dwelt on are in themselves suggestive. Six of Pennsylvania's eight delegates were

---

[32] Madison, "Vices," in *Papers of Madison*, vol. 9, pp. 345-358, also conveniently available in Marvin Meyers, ed., *The Mind of the Founder, Sources of the Political Thought of James Madison* (Indianapolis: Bobbs-Merrill, 1973), pp. 82-92.

[33] Most clearly explained in Madison to Jefferson, October 24, 1787, *Papers of Madison*, vol. 10, pp. 205-220.

members of the "Republican Constitutionalist" faction, fighting since 1777 to overturn their state's radical constitution (they did succeed in 1790). These included its leaders, James Wilson, Robert Morris, and Gouverneur Morris, then transient in Philadelphia. New York's delegation was composed of foes; on the one side, Hamilton, who had married into the New York landlord-commercial aristocracy, joining John Jay, James Duane, Robert R. Livingston and his father-in-law, Philip Schuyler, and, on the other side, John Lansing and Robert Yates, supporters of the Clintonian holders of state power that Hamilton despised. Maryland elected Charles Carroll, the younger, who was too preoccupied with internal state politics, it was said, to come; his cousin, Daniel Carroll, came, as did other members of the Carroll faction.[34]

Personal experience with democratic opponents did not automatically turn a conservative to the path of accommodation. The contrast is clear if one takes the two men who, next to Madison, are acknowledged as major shapers of the Constitution, Gouverneur Morris and Wilson. Morris never got over thinking about popular movements as animals requiring restraint. At the convention, he seems to have spoken consistently and often for the conservative solution to problems. Not only did he admire Hamilton's speech, he agreed with it: "We must have monarch sooner or later . . . and the sooner we take him, while we are able to make a bargain with him, the better."[35]

Wilson, on the other hand, although he had the searing experience in 1779 of having his house the target of an attack by the radical militia, was, as Robert McCloskey argues,

> more consistent than anyone else, including Madison, in advocating political democracy. He favored direct popular election of both Senate and House, and he joined with Madison in urging that the proposed Constitution be submitted to popularly elected conventions in each state. . . . But when Madison supported a freehold qualification for voting,

[34] Charles A. Beard, *An Economic Interpretation of the Constitution of the United States* (New York: Macmillan, 1913), chap. 7; Jackson Turner Main, *Political Parties Before the Constitution* (Chapel Hill: University of North Carolina Press, 1973); Forest McDonald, *We the People: The Economic Origins of the Constitution* (Chicago: University of Chicago Press, 1958); Robert L. Brunhouse, *The Counter Revolution in Pennsylvania, 1776-1790* (Harrisburg: Pennsylvania Historical Commission, 1942); Young, *Democratic Republicans of New York,* chaps. 1-5.

[35] Cited in Adair, *Fame and the Founding Fathers,* p. 119; see also Max Mintz, *Gouverneur Morris and the American Revolution* (Norman: University of Oklahoma Press, 1970), chap. 9; and for an array of extreme conservative proposals, Jane Butzner, comp., *Constitutional Chaff: Rejected Suggestions at the Constitutional Convention of 1787* (New York: Columbia University Press, 1941).

> Wilson opposed it, and Wilson was practically alone in argu-
> ing that the president too should be elected directly by the
> people. . . . Wilson stands forth as one of the most consistent
> democrats of his era.[36]

The accommodating cast of mind showed itself in the first week in the
debate over a resolution in the Virginia plan "that the members of the
first Branch of the national legislature ought to be elected by the
people of the several states" and not the state legislatures.[37] Elbridge
Gerry of Massachusetts, the memory of Shays' Rebellion fresh in his
mind, is often quoted for his remark:

> The evils we experience flow from an excess of democ-
> racy. . . . He had been too republican heretofore; He was still
> however republican, but had been taught by experience the
> danger of the levelling spirit.

The responses of George Mason of Virginia, Wilson, and Madison
were more typical:

> Mr. Mason argued strongly for an election of the larger
> branch by the people. It was to be the grand depository of
> the democratic principle of the Government. It was, so to
> speak, to be our House of Commons—It ought to know and
> sympathize with every part of the community. He admitted
> that we had been too democratic but was afraid we sd. incau-
> tiously run into the opposite extreme. We ought to attend
> to rights of every class of the people. . . .

Wilson "contended strenuously for drawing the most numerous
branch of the Legislature immediately from the people," revealing his
underlying assumptions:

> He was for raising the federal pyramid to a considerable
> altitude and for that reason wished to give it as broad a basis
> as possible. No government could long subsist without the
> confidence of the people.

Second,

> he also thought it wrong to increase the weight of the State
> Legislatures by making them the electors of the national
> Legislature. . . . On examination it would be found that the
> opposition of States to federal measures had proceeded much
> more from the Offices of the States than from the people at
> large.

---

[36] Robert G. McCloskey, ed., *The Works of James Wilson* (Cambridge, Mass.:
Harvard University Press, 1967), vol. 1, p. 5 and introduction.

[37] Farrand, ed., *Records*, vol. 1, pp. 47-53 for the quotations that follow.

Madison used a different metaphor: "The great fabric to be raised would be more stable and durable if it should rest on the solid foundation of the people themselves" than if it rested "merely on the pillars of the Legislatures." The problem was that in some states one branch was already elected indirectly; if the house were elected by such legislatures, "the people would be lost sight of altogether and the necessary sympathy between them and their rulers and officers, too little felt." He was, he made clear,

> an advocate for the policy of refining the popular appointments by successive filtrations, but thought it might be pushed too far. He wished the expedient to be resorted to only in the appointment of the second branch of the Legislature, and in the executive and judiciary branch of the Government.

Gerry then backtracked:

> Mr. Gerry did not like the election by the people. . . . Experience he said had shown that the State legislatures drawn immediately from the people did not always possess their confidence. He had no objection however to an election by the people if it were so qualified that men of honor and character might not be unwilling to be joined in the appointments. He seemed to think the people might nominate a certain number out of which the state legislatures should be bound to choose.

As one focuses on such a debate, as one probes for the assumptions underlying the debate as a whole, it seems one can differentiate five factors impelling the delegates in a democratic direction.

First, the underlying political theory to which the delegates subscribed dictated that, to survive in the long run, governments had to be adjusted to the mores and customs of the people to be governed (this was Montesquieu). The delegates were erecting a government "intended to last for ages," said Madison. "The British government cannot be our model," explained Wilson. "We have no materials for a similar one. Our manners, our laws, the abolition of entails and of primogeniture, the whole genius of the people, are opposed to it." Mason used the same term: "The genius of the people must be consulted."[38]

Second, one of the theoretical solutions to curbing the "vices" of democratic majorities in the states, an "extended republic," clearly led

---

[38] Ibid., pp. 48, 50 (Gerry), p. 431 (Madison), p. 153 (Wilson), p. 101 (Mason). See also ibid., p. 406 (Gorham).

in a democratic direction. This aspect of Madison's thought is so familiar there is no need to develop it here. At one point in presenting this theory, Madison even abandoned the term "republican" to argue that to "enlarge the sphere" was "the only defense against the inconvenience of *democracy* consistent with the democratic form of Government."[39] The immediate application of this theory was a house of representatives elected by popular vote. The long-range implication was the admission of new states to the union on a basis of equality that would "enlarge the sphere" still further. The argument needs no elaboration.

The second theoretical solution to the vices of the states, a national veto of state legislation, was equally undemocratic. Perhaps it is significant that Madison never achieved this in the form he wanted.

Third, the delegates recognized a short-term political reality. If the Constitution were to be adopted, it had to meet with popular approval. The convention could not submit it to the state legislatures—they were part of the problem. It therefore had to go to conventions whose delegates would be elected for the sole purpose of voting on the Constitution. Delegates were extremely sensitive to the "people out of doors." Pierce Butler, the South Carolina planter, put it well, in a response to a proposal to extend a federal judiciary into the states:

> The people will not bear such innovations. The states will revolt at such encroachments. Supposing such an establishment to be useful, we must not venture on it. We must follow the example of Solon who gave the Athenians not the best Government he could devise but the best they would receive.[40]

Fourth, there was an even more immediate political need to conciliate delegates "within doors." The delegates were hardly of one mind. Benjamin Franklin, for example, the nation's ornament, second in popularity only to Washington, was long a sympathizer with Pennsylvania's democratic constitution. As Clinton Rossiter has pointed out,

> [Franklin] would have preferred a constitution with these radically different arrangements: a plural executive, unsalaried and probably elected by the legislature; a unicameral legislature, with representation proportioned to population; annual elections for all holders of public office, including officers of the militia; universal manhood suffrage, with no

---

[39] Ibid., pp. 135-136.
[40] Ibid., p. 125.

bow to property; a straightforward, unqualified bill of rights; and an easy method of formal amendment.[41]

George Mason, the author of his state's bill of rights, was no less a sage in the eyes of Virginians. Yates and Lansing walked out; Mason, Randolph, Gerry, and Luther Martin stayed to the end but refused to sign. The chief architects labored to avoid such setbacks. They also had to placate a group of moderate nationalist delegates, in particular from New England.[42]

Nothing is more revealing of this self-imposed pressure to conciliate than Washington's action literally in the closing hour of the convention. Nathaniel Gorham of Massachusetts, "for the purpose of lessening objections to the constitution," moved to alter the number of representatives in the House from one for 40,000 inhabitants to one for 30,000; the number of representatives was a sore point with the democratic-minded. Washington left the chair—he had not spoken through the entire convention—"yet he could not forebear expressing his wish that the alteration proposed might take place. It was much to be desired that the objections to the plan recommended might be as few as possible."[43]

The fifth factor contributing to democratic results at the convention was the force of circumstance: diversity. Diversity led to bitter contention that almost rent the convention: the differences between the large and small states, between slaveholding and nonslaveholding states, cutting across the differences between agricultural and commercial interests. These differences led to the since classic compromises of the Constitution. At the same time, with issues affecting democracy such as qualifications for voting and officeholding, the diversity of political practice in the states produced a stalemate in which the delegates fell back on the solution of allowing each state to go its own way. The result in both the short run and long run was a democratic plus.

The debate on the suffrage may be taken as an example of how these several factors came into play, often explicitly, sometimes implicitly. This debate, late in the convention, was on the drafting committee's proposal for the election of members of the House by whomever each state allowed to vote for its "most numerous branch," that

---

[41] Clinton Rossiter, "The Political Theory of Benjamin Franklin," *The Pennsylvania Magazine of History and Biography* (July 1952), pp. 259-293.

[42] Cf. George Billias, *Elbridge Gerry: Founding Father and Republican Statesman* (New York: McGraw-Hill, 1976), chaps. 11-13, and, in general, Jensen, *The Revolution Within America*, chap. 4.

[43] Farrand, ed., *Records*, vol. 2, pp. 643-644.

is, the lower house. Gouverneur Morris characteristically moved to amend it, limiting the vote to freeholders, that is, farmers who owned their own farms, and explicitly requiring the national legislature rather than the states to determine the qualifications.[44] Morris, still trying to destroy the reptile, still discerning, sounded the traditional maxim that property was essential for an "independent" vote:

> Give the votes to people who have no property and they will sell them to the rich who will be able to buy them. We should not confine our attention to the present moment. The time is not distant when this Country will abound with mechanics and manufacturers who will receive their bread from their employers. . . . The man who does not give a vote freely is not represented. It is the man who dictates his vote. . . .

Madison expressed a similar fear, pointing to the cities as historic sources of corruption.

The opposition to Morris's amendment was broad and vigorous. Mason feared the short-term political consequences: "Eight or nine states have extended the right of suffrage beyond the freeholders, what will the people there say, if they should be disfranchised[?]" Oliver Ellsworth, chief justice of Connecticut, dwelt on the problem of diversity:

> How shall the freehold be defined? Ought not every man who pays a tax to vote for the representative who is to levy and dispose of his money? Shall the wealthy merchants and manufacturers, who will bear a full share of the public burdens be not allowed a voice in the imposition of them. . . .

The warmest opposition stemmed from delegates sensitive to urban constituencies in which the mass of mechanics already voted. Franklin, a man who had to be placated, made this one of the rare occasions at the convention when he spoke, paying a glowing tribute to "the lower class of Freemen" who would be disfranchised by a freehold requirement. "This class have hardy virtues and [great] integrity—the late war is a glorious testimony in favor of plebeian virtue." Wilson of Philadelphia dealt with realities:

> It was difficult to form any uniform rule of qualifications for all the States. . . . It would be very hard and disagreeable for the same persons at the same time, to vote for representatives in the State Legislature and to be excluded from a vote for those in the National Legislature.

---

[44] Ibid., vol. 2, pp. 201-206 and p. 225 for Gorham.

Nathaniel Gorham, a Boston merchant, pointedly answered Madison's claim that elections in the cities are unsafe. "The elections in Phila-[delphia] N[ew] York and Boston where the Merchants and Mechanics vote are at least as good as those made by freeholders only." As to the English experience, "the cities and large towns are not the seat of crown influence and corruption." Moreover, in America "the people" "will never allow [this right] to be abridged. We must consult their rooted prejudices if we expect their concurrence in our propositions."

Madison clearly was torn. He had no doubt that the issue should be resolved by the Constitution; "the right of suffrage is certainly one of the fundamental articles of republican Government, and ought not to be left to be regulated by the Legislature." But how? On the one hand was the short-term reality:

> Whether the Constitutional qualification ought to be a free-hold, would with him depend much on the probable reception such a change would meet with in States where the right was now exercised by every description of people. In several of the States a freehold was now the qualification.

On the other hand was the problem of long-run stability:

> Viewing the subject in its merits alone, the freeholders of the Country would be the safest depositiories of Republican liberty. In future times a great majority of the people will not only be without landed, but any other sort of, property. These will either combine under the influence of their common situation; in which case, the rights of property and the public liberty will not be secure in their hands; or which is more probable, they will become the tools of opulence and ambition, in which case there will be equal danger on another side.

In this speech he left his thought dangling; the thrust of it was clearly sympathetic to Morris and that is how others recorded it. In the balloting, Virginia voted against Morris's freehold amendment, and Madison's biographers presume he voted with his delegation. More than likely, the practical—"the probable reception" of such a proposal—overrode the theoretical—"viewing the subject in its merits alone."[45]

---

[45] Ibid., vol. 2, pp. 202-204; Irving Brant, *James Madison: Father of the Constitution, 1787-1800* (Indianapolis: Bobbs-Merrill, 1950), pp. 118-119; Ralph Ketcham, *James Madison, A Biography* (New York: Macmillan, 1971), pp. 220-221; for Madison's later thoughts on the suffrage, see Hutchinson et al., eds., *Papers of Madison*, vol. 10, pp. 140-141, and Farrand, ed., *Records*, vol. 3, pp. 450-455.

The freehold requirement was overwhelmingly defeated—seven states against, one in favor (Delaware), one divided (Maryland), one absent (Georgia). Not only would the suffrage remain fairly broad (and varied) as it was in 1787, but there would be nothing in the Constitution to prevent the states from broadening it. Three days later, a proposal to require property qualifications for members of the House and Senate "was rejected by so general a 'no' that the States were not called."[46] In such ways, diversity combined with political theory and political reality to produce a democratic result.

In looking at the Constitution as a whole, in measuring it on a spectrum of the revolutionary era in which Pennsylvania's constitution of 1776 stood at one end and Hamilton's proposal of June 1787, at the other, the federal end product was in the middle of the road. The argument has focused not on intentions but on a process by which the Founding Fathers did things "in spite of themselves," so to speak. They made democratic concessions to achieve conservative ends. They wanted a "broad basis" of popular support, because they intended to "raise the federal pyramid" so high. They wanted to "extend the sphere" to disperse the threat of democratic majorities.

They obviously got a good deal of what they wanted, but they also got less than they wanted. In a long letter to Jefferson shortly after the convention, Madison expressed what can only be called bitter disappointment at failing to achieve a federal veto of state legislation. "The restraints against paper emissions and violations of contracts" were "not sufficient" and were "short of the mark"; judicial review would only catch "mischiefs" after the fact. On the other hand, James Wilson, pointing to the same two curbs on the states, thought that "if only the following lines were inserted in this new constitution I think it would be worth our adoption." The chief architects themselves were divided—or of one opinion privately and another publicly. This, too, may be considered further testimony to the middle-of-the-road character of what they had wrought.[47]

---

[46] Farrand, ed., *Records*, vol. 2, p. 249; for a summary of the convention on suffrage, see Clinton Williamson, *American Suffrage from Property to Democracy, 1760-1860* (Princeton, N.J.: Princeton University Press, 1960), chap. 7.

[47] Madison to Jefferson, October 24, 1787, in Hutchinson et al., eds., *Papers of Madison*, vol. 10, pp. 205-220, and Charles F. Hobson, "The Negative on State Laws: James Madison, The Constitution and the Crisis of Republican Government," *William and Mary Quarterly*, 3rd ser., vol. 36 (April 1979), pp. 215-235, an important article challenging the notion that Madison's thoughts in *The Federalist* were identical with his private reactions to the Constitution.

Democratic Responses

Among those with a claim to being called democrats, the response to the Constitution in 1787–1788 was divided. Some opposed it; some gave it modified approval; some were enthusiastic supporters. Such division was what might be expected in response to a middle-of-the-road document.

Democrats who opposed the Constitution were to be found among the Antifederalists. Not all Antifederalists were democrats, a fact forcefully clarified by Cecilia Kenyon. In fact, in a very important way, the ideological tables of 1776 were turned. Men who in 1776 stressed a Paineite simple government, epitomized by a one-house legislature in which majorities would rule unchecked, now found the checks and balances in the national government inadequate. They did not take the ground that the progressive J. Allen Smith would take in 1906 and Charles Beard would repeat, namely that checks and balances were a means of thwarting democratic majorities. Indeed, they asked for more of them.[48]

The reversal was not all that inconsistent. Many democrats—if not most—had come around to accepting both bicameralism and the separation of powers. The New York Antifederalists, for example, probably agreed with their governor, George Clinton, that theirs was "our excellent state constitution." In 1790, many Pennsylvania democrats were to go along with the conservative restructuring of their state constitution.[49]

In 1787–1788, many democrats were convinced that a "consolidated" national government had been created by a few men of wealth whose excessive powers threatened the states. The starting point in their thinking about the Constitution among ordinary Antifederalists was a raw, gut feeling that the drafters and proponents of the new government were their class enemies. "An apprehension that the liberties of the people are in danger," said Rufus King of Massachu-

---

[48] Cecilia Kenyon, ed., *The Antifederalists* (Indianapolis: Bobbs-Merrill, 1966), introduction, and Kenyon, "Men of Little Faith: The Anti-Federalists on the Nature of Representative Government," *William and Mary Quarterly*, 3rd ser., vol. 12 (1955), pp. 3-43; J. Allen Smith, *The Spirit of American Government* (New York, 1907; reprinted Cambridge, Mass.: Harvard University Press, 1965, Cushing Strout, ed.). For Antifederalist democratic thought, see Jackson Turner Main, *The Anti-Federalists: Critics of the Constitution, 1781-88* (Chapel Hill: University of North Carolina Press, 1961), chaps. 6-8. I have also profited from reading the unpublished manuscript of the late Herbert Storing, "What the Anti-Federalists Were For," to be published as the introduction to Storing, ed., *The Complete Anti-Federalist* (University of Chicago Press, forthcoming).

[49] Young, *Democratic Republicans*, chap. 2, citation at p. 22. Brunhouse, *Counter Revolution in Pennsylvania*, chap. 7.

setts, "and a distrust of men of property and education have a more powerful effect upon the mind of our opponents than any specific objections against the Constitution."[50]

That frame of mind was summarized in one speech at the Massachusetts convention by Amos Singletary (a countryman from Worcester County, a self-taught man of whom it was said he "never attended school a day in his life" and who had served in the provincial congress and the assembly):

> These lawyers, and men of learning, and moneyed men, that talk so finely, and gloss over matters so smoothly, to make us poor illiterate people swallow down the pill, expect to get into congress themselves; they expect to be managers of this Constitution and get all the power and all the money into their own hands, and then they will swallow up all us little folks, like the great Leviathan, Mr. President; yes just as the whale swallowed up *Jonah*. This is what I am afraid of. . . .[51]

The political theory of such democratic Antifederalists was articulated well by Melancton Smith, the leading Antifederalist debater at New York's ratifying convention.[52] Smith developed his democratic assumptions in a clash over the number of representatives in the house, the issue that had led conservatives to a last-minute accommodation of one congressman for 30,000 instead of 40,000 voters. Smith moved one for 20,000. His concept of representation harked back to Paine:

> The idea that naturally suggests itself to our minds, when we speak of representatives, is, that they resemble those they represent. They should be a true picture of the people, possess a knowledge of their circumstances and their wants, sympathize in all their distresses, and be disposed to seek their true interests. The knowledge necessary for the representative of a free people not only comprehends extensive political and commercial information, such as is acquired by men of refined education, who have leisure to attain to high degrees of improvement, but it should also comprehend that

---

[50] King to Madison, cited in Samuel B. Harding, *The Contest over the Ratification of the Federal Constitution in the State of Massachusetts* (New York: Longmans, Green, 1896), pp. 78-79.

[51] Jonathan Elliot, comp., *The Debates in the Several State Conventions on the Adoption of the Federal Constitution*, 2d ed. (New York: Lippincott, 1888), vol. 2, pp. 101-102; Harding, ibid., p. 77n.

[52] Young, *Democratic Republicans*, pp. 48-49 and chap. 5; Robin Brooks, "Melancton Smith, New York Anti-Federalist," (Ph.D. thesis, University of Rochester, 1964), pp. 744-1,798, and Brooks, "Alexander Hamilton, Melancton Smith, and the Ratification of the Constitution in New York," *William and Mary Quarterly*, vol. 22 (1963), pp. 339-358.

kind of acquaintance with the common concerns and occupations of the people, which men of the middling class of life are, in general, more competent to than those of a superior class.[53]

Smith's underlying fear was that "the influence of the great will generally enable them to succeed in elections." They "easily form associations; the poor and middling class form them with great difficulty" and usually divide among themselves. As a result, "a substantial yeoman of sense and discernment will hardly ever be chosen" and the "government will fall into the hands of the few and the great."

An increase in the size of the house thus was crucial to permit democratic representation. In turning to the senate, Smith sought reforms to meet both his democratic assumptions of representation and his fears for the state governments. He argued for the rotation and recall of senators; they should be eligible to serve only six years in any twelve-year period. Recall was necessary because senators were "the representatives of state legislatures. . . . When a state sends an agent commissioned to transact any business, or perform any services, it certainly ought to have a power to recall." He spoke for an amendment to limit the president to one term, which he was willing to lengthen to seven years. He also wanted the president's military powers and powers of appointment curbed. To restrain the federal judicial power, Smith favored a series of curtailing amendments.[54]

The New York convention, under Smith's leadership, adopted a long series of amendments that would have seriously altered the structure of the federal government. Later, when the Bill of Rights amendments alone were passed, Abraham Yates, the stormy petrel of New York Antifederalism, pronounced them "unimportant or trivial" compared to what was sought.[55]

We may let Thomas Jefferson speak for those moderate democrats who gave the Constitution qualified support and rapidly swallowed their objections. This generation is sanguine about the limitations of Jefferson's aristocratic liberalism: the darker side of his record on civil liberties, his failures on slavery and racial equality, his own insistence that the practical must control the theoretical. On reflection,

---

[53] Elliot, ed., *Debates*, vol. 2, pp. 243-251, 259-260.

[54] Ibid., pp. 310-311, 407-411; see Theophilius Parsons, Jr., "The Old Convictions and the New Realities: New York Anti-federalists and the Radical Whig Tradition" (Ph.D. thesis, Columbia University, 1974).

[55] Elliot, ed., *Debates*, vol. 2, pp. 327-331 for the amendments; Abraham Yates, Rough Hewer Notebooks, March 15, 22, 1790, Yates Papers, New York Public Library, reprinted in Young, ed., *The Debate Over the Constitution, 1787-1789* (Chicago: Rand McNally, 1965), pp. 44-46.

he still qualifies as a democrat, albeit a moderate one compared to, say, a Philadelphia militia man. A Whig, an advocate of balanced government and the separation of powers, he was nonetheless a severe critic of the gross inequality of representation in Virginia. However much he hedged his faith in the people, he had an uncommon confidence in popular majorities.[56]

Throughout the convention, Jefferson was in Paris as America's minister to France. Predisposed to a stronger government, he was surprisingly hostile in his initial reactions to the Constitution. There were "things in it which stagger all my dispositions to subscribe to it." "All the good," he wrote John Adams, "might have been couched in three or four new articles to be added to the good, old and venerable fabric, the Articles of Confederation, which should even have been preserved as a religious relic." "I find myself nearly a neutral," he wrote another. "There is a great mass of good in it, in a very desirable form; but there is also to be a bitter pill or two." When Paine arrived in Paris, he, Jefferson, and the marquis de Lafayette debated the document "in a convention of our own as earnestly as if we were to decide upon it," Lafayette said.[57]

Gradually Jefferson softened. To Madison, he couched his thoughts as "what I like" and "what I do not like." He liked the idea of the central government "which should go on of itself peaceably, without needing continual recurrence to the state legislatures," the three branches in the federal government, the power of the House to vote taxes, and "the negative given to the executive with a third of either house," although he would have liked the judiciary to be involved. In short, the moderate democrat did not balk at a national government, at separation of powers, presidential veto, or even judicial review.

What he did not like was, "first, the omission of a bill of rights," a point on which he belabored Madison at length and with passion. "A second feature" he "greatly disliked" "is the abandonment of the necessity of rotation in office, and most particularly in the case of the President." He was convinced that "the first magistrate will always be reelected. . . . He is then an officer for life." He feared this espe-

---

[56] Leonard Levy, *Jefferson and Civil Liberties: The Darker Side* (Cambridge, Mass.: Harvard University Press, 1963); Winthrop Jordan, *White Over Black: American Attitudes Towards the Negro, 1550-1812* (Chapel Hill: University of North Carolina Press, 1968), chap. 12; Merrill Peterson, *Thomas Jefferson and the New Nation: A Biography* (New York: Oxford University Press, 1970).

[57] Jefferson to John Adams, November 13, 1787, to William S. Smith, November 13, 1787, to Edward Carrington, December 21, 1787, in Boyd, ed., *Papers of Thomas Jefferson*, vol. 12, pp. 349-351, 355-357, 445-447; Lafayette cited in Louis Gottschalk, *Lafayette Between the American and French Revolution, 1783-1789* (Chicago: University of Chicago Press, 1950), p. 374.

cially because of the danger of the influence of foreign nations. "An incapacity to be elected a second time" was "the only effectual preventative." These were his likes and dislikes.[58]

It was characteristic of Jefferson that in the same letter to Madison he turned from the Constitution to Shays' Rebellion, giving another admonition against repression that might smother the spirit of liberty: "I own I am not a friend to very energetic government. It is always oppressive." It was especially characteristic of his political thinking that he concluded by saying he would agree with the majority on the Constitution. "After all it is my principle that the will of the majority should always prevail. If they should approve the proposed Constitution in all its parts, I shall concur in it cheerfully, in hopes that they will amend it whenever they shall find it works wrong." In effect, he saw no obstacle to a majority in the amending process.

To force a bill of rights, Jefferson would have preferred ratification by less than the required states, but, once ratification occurred, he shifted rapidly. Soon the Constitution was "unquestionably the wisest ever yet presented to men" and *The Federalist* the "best commentary on the principles on government, which was ever written."[59] The fact that Jefferson could change, and change so rapidly, the fact that so many Antifederalists could also learn to live with the Constitution may well be considered testimony to the powerful pull of the democratic features of the document.

The democrats who gave the Constitution enthusiastic backing— the third type of democrat of the period—were the artisans of the major cities. Support was overwhelming from all but a small minority of the mechanic classes. In Philadelphia, the vote for convention delegates averaged about 1,200 for the Federalists to about 150 for the Antifederalists. In New York, with universal male suffrage prevailing, the vote was 2,700 to 150. In Boston, where mechanic voters in the town meeting elected an Antifederalist ticket headed by Samuel Adams, their traditional spokesman, mechanic pressure turned Adams around from nay to yea.[60]

[58] Jefferson to Madison, December 20, 1787, in Boyd, ed., *The Papers of Jefferson*, vol. 12, pp. 439-442.

[59] Jefferson to David Humphreys, March 18, 1789, cited in Dumas Malone, *Jefferson and the Rights of Man* (Boston: Little, Brown, 1951), p. 178 and see chap. 9; Jefferson to Madison, 1788 (on *The Federalist*), cited in Richard Hofstadter, *The American Political Tradition and the Men Who Made It* (New York: Knopf, 1948), p. 30.

[60] Staughton Lynd, "The Mechanics in New York Politics, 1774-1788," *Labor History*, vol. 5 (1968), pp. 225-246; Charles Olton, *Artisans for Independence: Philadelphia Mechanics and the American Revolution* (Syracuse: Syracuse University Press, 1975), chap. 9.

In 1776, artisans had supported democratic constitutional reform. On what basis did they support the Constitution of 1787? Paine gives us some clues. He came as close as any man to being a spokesman for urban artisans and a hero to them. Paine was unquestionably a democrat; he defended the beleaguered Pennsylvania constitution as "good for a poor man." From the outset of the Revolution he was also a nationalist. *Common Sense* had called for a nationally elected assembly, and Paine, at the center of the effort to mobilize support for the war, was always keenly aware of the inadequacies of the confederation. "The continental belt is too loosely buckled," he put it. Postwar experiences only strengthened this conviction. As Britain dumped manufactures in America, as commerce stagnated, keeping shipbuilding at a low ebb, artisans promoted vigorous demands for tariff protection and the promotion of commerce. Meanwhile, nationalist business leaders like Robert Morris sought support for bank charters; all nationalists sought a source of independent revenue for the federal government. In Paine, all these movements converged. By 1786, in most cities an alliance of artisans and merchants was a reality.[61]

In France, Paine's response to the Constitution was similar to Jefferson's. There was a compelling need for national union. "Thirteen staves and ne'er a hoop will not make a barrel," he later wrote; "any kind of hooping the barrel, however defectively executed would be better than none." Paine boasted that as early as 1776 *Common Sense* called for "a convention to form a continental association" and that, in 1782, he had made the same proposal in a letter to Robert R. Livingston, then minister of foreign affairs. He was not ashamed to admit that he had a meeting to discuss it with Livingston, Robert Morris, and Gouverneur Morris—all of whom, we might add, found the constitution of Pennsylvania "bad for a rich man."[62]

Paine's criticism of the Constitution resembled Jefferson's only in the absence of a bill of rights. He objected to the presidency. He had "always been opposed," he explained, "to a single executive." "A plurality is far better. It combines the mass of a nation better together. And besides this, it is necessary to the manly mind of a republic that it loses the debasing idea of obeying an individual." He objected also to "the long duration of the Senate," and he seems to

---

[61] Foner, *Tom Paine*, chap. 6; for the political shifts in Philadelphia, see Owen Ireland, "Partisanship and the Constitution: Pennsylvania, 1787," *Pennsylvania History*, vol. 45 (1978), pp. 328-332, and George Bryan, "An Account of the Adoption of the Constitution of 1787," George Bryan Papers, Historical Society of Pennsylvania (brought to my attention by Steven Rosswurm).

[62] Paine, "A Letter to George Washington, July 30, 1796" in P. Foner, ed., *Complete Writings of Paine*, vol. 2, pp. 691-693.

have had misgivings, not explained, as to the general framework of the federal government. The Constitution was "a copy, though not quite so base as the original, of the form of the British Government."

The saving grace in the Constitution, for Paine as for Jefferson, was the possibility of amending it:

> It was only the absolute necessity of establishing some Federal authority extending equally over all the States, that an instrument so inconsistent as the present Federal Constitution is, obtained a suffrage. I would have voted for it myself, had I been in America, or even for a worse, rather than have none, provided it contained the means of remedying its defects by the same appeal to the people by which it was to be established. It is always a better policy to leave removable errors to expose themselves than to hazard too much in contending against them theoretically.[63]

If artisans had any of Paine's misgivings about the Constitution, they left no record of them. They made their political thought clear in a form not usually "read" by students of political thought—the massive parades celebrating ratification in 1788, the largest parades in American history to that time: Boston, 4,000 marchers; New York, 5,000; Philadelphia, 5,000 to 6,000; Charleston, 2,800; and proportionate numbers in lesser cities like Baltimore, Annapolis, Savannah, New Haven, and Portsmouth. Mechanics, who composed from one-half to two-thirds of the adult males in the cities, were easily that proportion of the marchers. The parades were arranged by city officials or politicians, often with mechanics participating on the general planning committees and meeting separately to plan their participation. They were hardly coerced—indeed, as Richard Morris has observed, ratification was "joyfully greeted by working-class people in every city in the Land."[64]

What do the parades show us? First, they showed craft consciousness, an overwhelming pride of craft. "By Hammer and Hand All Arts Do Stand" was the official slogan of the General Society of Mechanics and Tradesmen of New York; each trade expressed this. Mechanics marched by trades, arranged either alphabetically from bakers to wheelwrights, or by "branch" in separate units, for example, the building trades or the leather trades. Masters marched at the head of journeymen and apprentices. Each trade displayed either a fin-

---

[63] Ibid., p. 691.

[64] Whitefield Bell, Jr., "The Federalist Processions of 1788," *New York Historical Society Quarterly*, vol. 46 (1962), pp. 5-39; Morris, "We the People of the United States," p. 15; the quotations following are taken from a variety of contemporary sources.

ished product dubbed with an appropriate name, as the bakers with a huge "Federal Loaf" of bread or a float on which men plied their trade, as the coopers making a barrel, hooping thirteen staves together, or the printers casting off copies of the Constitution from a press. In almost every large city, a feature was a miniature ship mounted on wheels drawn by teams of horses, built by ship carpenters, variously called "The Ship of State," "The Constitution," or, in New York, "The Hamilton." Artisans displayed banners with the traditional symbols of their trade, repeating the coats of arms of London guilds or allegorical symbols establishing the antiquity of the craft, such as the tailors with a banner of Adam and Eve properly covered with fig leaves and a slogan, "They did sew fig leaves together."

Second, artisans, by the slogans on their banners, made clear that they had views on political economy. Blacksmiths and nailers spoke for protection for manufacturers:

> While Industry prevails
> We need no foreign nails.

The chairmakers wanted new markets for the export of manufactures:

> The Federal States in union bound
> O'er all the world our chairs are found.

The shipwrights sought expanding commerce:

> This federal ship will our commerce revive
> And merchants and shipwrights and joiners shall thrive.

Last, their slogans and symbols suggest the larger political aspirations they saw fulfilled by the Constitution. The bricklayers' was "Both Buildings and rulers are the work of our hands." The printers with a portrait of Benjamin Franklin as their symbol, had the motto, "Where liberty dwells there is my country." The tallow chandlers rallied to "The stars of America, a light to the world." The upholsterers carried an elegant "Federal chair of state," supported by symbols of Liberty and Justice, "to the right a comely lad in the character of Liberty, supporting in his right hand the staff and cap of liberty, on the left another handsome lad bearing in his right hand the sword of justice and in his left the balance."

Clearly, to all these artisans, the Constitution was the fulfillment of the spirit of 1776, not its negation. Protection for American manufactures was a leitmotif of the mechanics movement from the first boycotts of British goods in the 1760s. The right to participate in political life—a voice, recognition, respect—was the *sine qua non* of their democratic aspirations. The Constitution guaranteed the suffrage advances of the revolutionary era. Moreover, there was something in the very process by which the Constitution had been adopted—a convention, submission to the people, discussion, the election of delegates —that ran very close to the conception advanced in 1776 by Paine in *Common Sense* and by the New York mechanics.* They must have seen in the Constitution itself an opportunity for the continued expression of their aspirations.[65]

If we return, after this long excursion into the revolutionary era, to Hamilton's proposal at the Philadelphia Convention, it is not at all hard to see why it was rejected. It went too far: too far in "extinguishing" the states; too far toward a King, House of Lords, House of Commons. Hamilton was too astute not to realize it. He later said he knew it "went beyond the ideas of most members" but "it was brought forward to make it the subject of discussion," "not as a thing attainable by us, but as a model which we ought to approach as near as possible."[66]

A month later, Hamilton was back with a second plan, somewhat less "high-toned." At the end, he signed the document, insisting with some accuracy that it was "remote" from his own.[67] He then joined Madison to write *The Federalist Papers*, putting the Constitution in its most republican light. At the New York convention, he fought for ratification on the same basis; "he is quite a republican," said an Antifederalist ("but he is known").[68] There he pleaded for the same "spirit of accommodation" that had "governed the convention" in Philadelphia.[69] Thus, in his own way, it could be argued, Hamilton's actions proved that he too was an accommodating conservative, or, at the least, that he was part of a process of accommodation to democratic pressures that was the legacy of the Founding Fathers to subsequent generations of conservatives.

---

[65] Alfred F. Young, " 'By Hammer and Hand All Arts do Stand'; The Mechanic Classes and the Shaping of the American Nation, 1760-1820, An Interpretation," (Paper delivered at a meeting of the Organization of American Historians, San Francisco, April 1980).

[66] Hamilton, "To the New York Evening Post," February 24, 1802, in Syrett, ed., *Hamilton Papers*, vol. 26, pp. 536-539 (brought to my attention by Morton Frisch); see also Mitchell, *Hamilton*, vol. 1, pp. 394-395.

[67] Ibid., p. 399, and "Draft of a Constitution," in Syrett, ed., *Hamilton Papers*, vol. 4, pp. 253-274; "Remarks on Signing," ibid., p. 253.

[68] Young, *Democratic Republicans*, chap. 5, citation at p. 113.

[69] Eliot, ed., *Debates*, vol. 2, p. 237.

---

* For another view of the ratification process and the question of popular support for the Constitution, see Michael Parenti's essay in this volume—Eds.

The Editors and the Authors

ROBERT A. GOLDWIN is a resident scholar and director of constitutional studies at the American Enterprise Institute. He served in the White House as special consultant to the president and, concurrently, as adviser to the secretary of defense. He taught at the University of Chicago and Kenyon College and was the dean of St. John's College in Annapolis. His edited books include *How Democratic Is America?*; *Left, Right and Center*; and *Political Parties in the Eighties*.

WILLIAM A. SCHAMBRA is assistant director of constitutional studies at the American Enterprise Institute and was associate editor of AEI's *Public Opinion* magazine. He is editing a collection of essays by the late Martin Diamond, a preeminent scholar of constitutional studies.

WALTER BERNS is a resident scholar at the American Enterprise Institute and professorial lecturer in constitutional law at Georgetown University. He is the author of *Freedom, Virtue and the First Amendment*; *The First Amendment and the Future of American Democracy*; and *For Capital Punishment*, and numerous articles in professional journals and popular magazines on constitutional issues. He has served as professor of political science at Yale, Cornell, and the University of Toronto.

JOSEPH M. BESSETTE is a professor of political science at Catholic University. He is a coprincipal investigator on a study sponsored by the National Endowment for the Humanities entitled "Rhetoric and Presidential Leadership" and a coeditor of and contributor to *The Presidency in the Constitutional Order*, forthcoming.

ANN STUART DIAMOND is assistant director of AEI's legal policy studies program. She has taught at Georgetown University, Yale University,

Rockford College, Claremont Men's College, and the University of Denver. Her most recent article, "The Zenith of Separation of Powers Theory: The Federal Convention of 1787," appeared in *Publius, The Journal of Federalism*, Summer 1978.

Wilson Carey McWilliams is professor of political science, Livingston College, Rutgers University. Among his publications are *The Idea of Fraternity in America*; "American Pluralism," in *The Americans, 1976*, edited by Irving Kristol and Paul Weaver; and "Civil Disobedience and Contemporary Constitutionalism," in *Comparative Politics*.

Michael Parenti is a visiting fellow at the Institute for Policy Studies and an adjunct professor of political science at American University. He is the author of numerous articles on American political and social life. Among his most recent books are *Democracy for the Few* and *Power and the Powerless*.

Gordon S. Wood is professor of history at Brown University. He formerly taught at Harvard University and the University of Michigan. His book *The Creation of the American Republic, 1776–1787* was awarded the Bancroft Prize by Columbia University and the John H. Dunning Prize by the American Historical Association. His most recent book is *The Great Republic: A History of the American People*.

Alfred F. Young is professor of history at Northern Illinois University and general editor (with Leonard W. Levy) of *The American Heritage Series*. He has written many books, papers, and articles on early American history including *The Democratic Republicans of New York: The Origins, 1763–1797* and *The Crowd and the Coming of the American Revolution: From Ritual to Rebellion in Boston, 1745–1775*.

A Note on the Book

The typeface used for the text of this book is Palatino, designed by Herman Zapf. The type was set by Hendricks-Miller Typographic Company, of Washington, D.C. Book-Crafters, Inc., of Chelsea, Michigan, printed and bound the book, using Glatfelter paper. The cover and format were designed by Pat Taylor.

The manuscript was edited by Ann Petty and by Margaret Seawell, of the AEI Publications staff.

SELECTED AEI PUBLICATIONS

Public Opinion, published bimonthly (one year, $12; two years, $22; single copy, $2.50)

The Presidential Nominating Process: Can It Be Improved? Jeane J. Kirkpatrick, Michael J. Malbin, Thomas E. Mann, Howard R. Penniman, and Austin Ranney (27 pp., $3.25)

Vital Statistics on Congress, 1980, John F. Bibby, Thomas E. Mann, Norman J. Ornstein (113 pp., paper $5.25, cloth $12.25)

Presidents and Prime Ministers, Richard Rose and Ezra N. Suleiman, eds. (347 pp., $8.25)

Democracy and Mediating Structures: A Theological Inquiry, Michael Novak, ed. (216 pp., paper $7.25, cloth, $13.25)

Future Directions for Public Policy, John Charles Daly, mod. (38 pp., $3.75)

Political Parties in the Eighties, Robert A. Goldwin, ed. (152 pp., paper $5.25, cloth $10.25)

Bureaucrats, Policy Analysts, Statesmen: Who Leads? Robert A. Goldwin, ed. (134 pp., paper $5.25, cloth $10.25)

The French National Assembly Elections of 1978, Howard R. Penniman, ed. (255 pp., $7.25)

A Conversation with Gerald R. Ford: Thoughts on Economics and Politics in the 1980s (19 pp., $2.25)

Prices subject to change without notice.

AEI ASSOCIATES PROGRAM

The American Enterprise Institute invites your participation in the competition of ideas through its AEI Associates Program. This program has two objectives:

The first is to broaden the distribution of AEI studies, conferences, forums, and reviews, and thereby to extend public familiarity with the issues. AEI Associates receive regular information on AEI research and programs, and they can order publications and cassettes at a savings.

The second objective is to increase the research activity of the American Enterprise Institute and the dissemination of its published materials to policy makers, the academic community, journalists, and others who help shape public attitudes. Your contribution, which in most cases is partly tax deductible, will help ensure that decision makers have the benefit of scholarly research on the practical options to be considered before programs are formulated. The issues studied by AEI include:

- Defense Policy
- Economic Policy
- Energy Policy
- Foreign Policy
- Government Regulation

- Health Policy
- Legal Policy
- Political and Social Processes
- Social Security and Retirement Policy
- Tax Policy

For more information, write to: AMERICAN ENTERPRISE INSTITUTE
1150 Seventeenth Street, N.W.
Washington, D.C. 20036